NO HAPPY ENDINGS

ALSO BY NORA McINERNY

It's Okay to Laugh

NO HAPPY ENDINGS

A Memoir

Nora McInerny

DEY ST.
An Imprint of WILLIAM MORROW

These are stories about my life, told how I remember them. Sometimes I changed names, and sometimes I didn't. If you remember these stories differently, good for you!

Art on page 262 by Chelsea Brink and reprinted with permission.

DEY ST.

NO HAPPY ENDINGS. Copyright © 2019 by Nora McInerny. All rights reserved. Printed in the United States of America. No part of this book may be used or reproduced in any manner whatsoever without written permission except in the case of brief quotations embodied in critical articles and reviews. For information, address HarperCollins Publishers, 195 Broadway, New York, NY 10007.

HarperCollins books may be purchased for educational, business, or sales promotional use. For information, please email the Special Markets Department at SPsales@harpercollins.com.

FIRST EDITION

Designed by Michelle Crowe

Library of Congress Cataloging-in-Publication Data has been applied for.

ISBN 978-0-06279240-2

19 20 21 22 23 DIX/LSC 10 9 8 7 6 5 4 3 2 1

For Aaron.
For Matthew.
For Ian.
For Sophie.
For Ralph.
For Baby.
For love.

CONTENTS

Introduction

The question came from the back of the room and hung in the air long after it had been asked. The tone was hopeful and anticipatory, as if the asker thought she was opening a gift for the entire audience.

"Are you . . . pregnant?"

It was asked with a beaming smile, with all of the joyful and elated body language you can imagine. But the words hit me like a grenade. The room was silent while I blinked and breathed in.

The question went unanswered until one of the other hundred attendees mercifully raised her hand, and lobbed me something more related to my actual talk, which was called, in all truthful irony, "Owning Your Own Story." I had just spent over an hour talking about the most painful period of my life: how my husband and my father died just weeks after my miscarriage. My husband was thirty-five when brain cancer finally killed him, my father sixty-four when he died of cancer of the Everything. In the aftermath of these monumental losses, I'd written a book, established a nonprofit retail brand, and started a podcast.

I'd also fallen in love again, and yes, I *was* pregnant, and these two new parts of life were fact, but they had also filled me with a deep ambivalence and a splash of shame that I had no interest in talking about with a hundred strangers, or even a hundred friends. Or even one friend. I didn't want to talk about it with anybody. I *thought* everyone knew that it was one thousand percent inappropriate to ask a woman if she was pregnant. Especially a woman who has publicly shared her pregnancy loss. Especially a woman who has publicly shared her pregnancy loss and is now standing in intentionally loose clothing in front of approximately a hundred strangers just a year and a half after her husband died. All this inquisitor knew was that I looked a little puffy in the face and a little thick in the midsection, and that I'd posted a few times about a man I was dating.

I hadn't hidden my relationship with Matthew, but I was more private about it than most people who fall deeply in love. He'd met my family, and my few close friends. Most people in this blissful state can't help but scream it from the rooftops and all forms of social media. I didn't post photos of Matthew very often, and when I did, I didn't use his name. Anyone who followed me on social media would be under the impression I was dating someone. That I was happy. They most certainly would not know that we were full-on in love, were blending our families, and that I was now gestating a fresh human.

I did this partially because Matthew is the kind of person for whom the internet is simply a utility: a font of information and nothing more. He has the supernatural ability to look at his phone *only when he needs to*, and the idea of posting something about his life on the internet in a way that strangers can view is a concept he cannot grasp. So yes, I was partially trying to respect his privacy, but I was *mostly* trying to protect myself. From the judgment of others, which was primarily just a projection of my own self-judgment. There was a version of me that thought loving another person would somehow diminish the love I still felt for Aaron. A version of me that thought that if I was happy, I must not be sad anymore, and if I wasn't sad anymore, then I guess I didn't love Aaron as much as I said I did. Or maybe that my new happiness was ill-gotten, a well-made fake, something I swiped off the back of a truck when nobody was looking.

This is what life looks like when you water the seeds of joy with guilt and shame. It feels as good as it sounds.

When bad things happen to you—a death, an illness, a divorce, a job loss—you quickly go from being a person to being just a sad story. I know from experience that *nobody* wants to be a sad story, and that no matter what you've been through, your story is always so much more than *just* sad. And your happy stories are more than just *happy*. Obviously, everything is more complicated than it appears on Instagram. But it is incredibly difficult to *live* with complicated. It is even more difficult for other people to *deal* with complicated.

"Are you pregnant?"

This stranger didn't know that she had pushed me into a rabbit hole of shame with her question. She was giving me a chance to tell everyone about my happy ending, about how the struggle and the loss was all worth it. But that's oversimplifying the narrative. I couldn't talk about my happiness without touching the uncomfortable truth that everything I have now is built on everything I lost. That I wouldn't have this book, my last book, a podcast, this baby, my man, and this big, blended family if I hadn't first lost Aaron, and my dad, and that second baby. That the trade would never seem fair, no matter how much I love Matthew or this baby or this family of ours. I could never say I'd rather have one version of my family over the other.

In certain widow circles, they call falling in love again your Chapter 2. It's not a whole new life, or a whole new story; it's the continuation of something else. But death is not the only time that we start over. Life is flexible and has long legs and a million different ways to kick you right in the chops. We lose the ones we love, but we also lose friends, jobs, and our sense of self. And then, we get to assemble something new from whatever is left behind.

My new life was me, and Ralph, and whatever we chose to make from the rubble of the life we had with Aaron. I could have sifted through the wreckage and tried to make a reasonable recreation of what we had, but it would have been obviously broken, obviously wrong. I didn't want a knockoff of my old life with just one less family member. I didn't want to pretend to be a normal person with normal worries.

I wasn't a normal person. I was a person who had seen beyond the veil, who had watched a young and vibrant person fade into what comes next. I didn't know what I was supposed to make of this new life, but I knew what I wasn't supposed to do, and knowing what *not* to do is a fine place to start.

If you read the fine print, you will find that life is subject to change without notice. I did not fill up my tragedy punch card with a dead husband, a dead parent, and a lost pregnancy. Tragedy is like a BOGO that never ends, for things you never wanted. It's a terrible deal, but it's not up for negotiating. The acknowledgment that when bad things happen they can just keep happening holds a lot of power. It can shut you down or open you up. Nobody would blame you for shutting yourself around your hurt, your loss. Nobody would blame you for making you or your life smaller, for rolling up like a threatened armadillo, which is my default reflex. A reflex, though, is not a choice. But the flip side of tragedy can be happiness. And that comes in waves, too. Thank God.

"Wait," you may be thinking, an eye roll at the ready, "is this entire book going to be about this lady complaining about how sad she is that she got to fall in love twice?" Well. No. That's not what the *entire* book is about! I'm in love again. With two men, now. I'm basically a polygamist, but nobody can put me in jail for it because one of them is dead. I'm a mom to two, a stepmom to two more, and a dog mom to one.*

I'm happy but I don't have my perfect Hollywood happy ending. Because it isn't always happy, and it isn't the end. This is life after life after life, in all of the chaos and contradiction of feelings and doings and beings involved. There will be unimaginable joy and incomprehensible tragedy. There will be endings. But there will be no happy endings.

---

* "Dog mom" was my dead dad's least favorite term but I'm not afraid to say that I am deeply in love with my dog and I don't care who knows it!!!

Chapter One

How to Have a Total Breakdown

So, you think you're ready to have a breakdown, do ya? Well, take it from a woman who has spent more than one afternoon sobbing in her minivan in the Costco parking lot: you're probably closer than you think you are. And if not, getting there won't be as hard as you think. All you need to get started are a few simple elements you can find laying around in your own heart. Ready, set, breakdown!

1. AN INCITING INCIDENT

And an exciting one, too! What's the worst that could happen? Maybe a spouse or a parent could die. Maybe you lose your job or end a relationship. There are many ways for your life to fall apart, and if you're lucky, one will come flying at you with no effort on your part. Now, if these situations aren't available to you, create one! Become so irritable and controlling that the people you love have no choice but to distance themselves from you, perhaps citing your "toxic nature." If you have a job, stop doing it! Or show up and do a really *bad* job. However you choose to jump-start the situation yourself, know that the real fun begins only after the disaster.

2. **BE "FINE"**

How *are* you? Well, you're *fine*, of course! You've never been better. I mean, sure, those medical bills are adding up to more than your house is worth, and yeah, you're not on "speaking terms" with your siblings, and no, you don't exactly have a job, but overall? When you think of it? Ya can't complain. Turn the conversation back onto the asker as soon as humanly possible. You'll immediately find out that they're just as fine as you are. Wild, right?

3. **DI(ALL)Y**

Help? Who needs help? Not you. You can handle it. Totally. Whatever *it* is. Three hours in line at the Social Security office, only to find out that your form wasn't notarized on the third day of the month with Saturn in your fifth house? Not a problem. Two kids with the stomach flu and a job that doesn't give you paid sick time? You *got* this. A burning pit of despair growing stronger every day like the Eye of Sauron? All over it. Those cracks you're starting to feel in that Totally Fine Construct you worked so hard on? That's the breakdown coming. The cortisol is pumping, your blood pressure is banging, and your body, which doesn't know the difference between emotional stress and being chased by a sabre-toothed tiger, is *freaking the fudge out*. Delicious, isn't it? Don't worry, there's more where that came from!

4. **DOUBLE YOUR STANDARDS**

Where the heck have all your friends and family gone? It's almost like when you told them you were fine and didn't need any help, they *believed* you? Are they nuts? Have they totally lost it? Aren't they listening to you? How could they not see your suffering, just because you carefully concealed it under Instagram filters and quality lipsticks? It's very important that you don't verbalize any of this to them, of course. This pain is a secret you must bury deep inside, and water with resentment and anxiety. Let it grow into a grudge, then blossom into a freak-out. You're almost there.

5. **CRACK!**

It's an onomatopoeia (that took me five attempts to spell correctly before giving up and just letting autocorrect do the job it was born to do), and the whole purpose behind this exercise. The timeline will look different for everyone, but that being said, it should take you no more than a year to get to this point. A year is a good milestone. After a year, most people stop caring about whatever it is that happened in your life. Not because they're awful people (though some of them are) but because their lives are also pretty lifey, and you and your tragedy has slid off the bottom of their To Care About list.

If this step does take you more than a year, you'll want to really take a good look at how you performed steps 1 to 3, because you didn't do them right. If you've interfered with this process with meditation, prayer, therapy, or mood stabilizers, well then, you have nobody to blame but yourself for your tragically healthy mental state. Otherwise, you can expect that constant burning rage you've been stoking inside of you to come bursting out of you very soon, likely when you least expect it. Maybe your brother will say something that the rest of your family hears as a joke, but *you* hear correctly as a vicious dig on you and everything you stand for. Perhaps someone who appears to be just driving to work, probably zoned out and listening to public radio, is actually trying to run you off the road and kill you in a fiery wreck and you'll be forced to drive up beside them and scream at the top of your lungs while shooting them double-barrel middle fingers. Perhaps you'll be sitting in your driveway, trying to steal a few blessed moments alone in your car before you walk into your house and whatever comes next, and an old Cher song will come on the radio. It's a dance tune, but when she asks if you believe in life after love? And suggests that inside her, something is saying she isn't strong enough? You *relate. Strongly.*

Most likely, the woman behind you at Target will be chewing her gum too loud while her husband loudly espouses his questionable political beliefs.

In any of these instances, you will leave your body, hovering above yourself while you breathe enough fire to burn any remaining bridges to sanity you may have. When you come back to your body, back to the full consciousness of what you've done, and what you've been through, you'll feel it. It's cold and icy and dark and heavy. It's the unmistakable knowledge that everything is as broken as you thought it was.

Especially you.

Chapter Two

You Need Therapy

My answers to the patient questionnaire went like this:

1. Always

2. Always

3. Constantly

4. Daily

5. 10 out of 10

6. 10 out of 10

7. Yes

8. Absolutely

9. Mmhmm

10. Daily

*　　*　　*

THERE MAY HAVE BEEN MORE questions, but the doctor could have just as easily filled out the sheet as if she were a kid who hadn't studied for the SATs and had decided to just fill out the D bubble for every answer. She took a few moments to tally up the score and gave me the results. I got an A! And a D! Anxiety *and* Depression. Good job, me!

I HADN'T SEEN A DOCTOR since my miscarriage. There may have been a check-up right after, but I don't remember it, not unexpected given the grief fog I was in. A check-up seemed like something that a well-adjusted, functional adult should do, even if it was a few months late, so I picked a doctor who had an office near me and booked an appointment.

We'd done our introductions and shaken hands when she asked if we'd met before. If you grew up in Minneapolis, there is a strong chance that we *have* met before, and this doctor and I were around the same age. Maybe our moms or our dads had gone to high school together? Maybe we played rec league basketball against each other in fifth grade and I fouled her a lot? We did the usual name game, and decided nope, we'd never met. It was probably just one of those things. There are a lot of tall blond women in Minneapolis, and I'm often mistaken for any number of them.

I loved this doctor right away. She gently touched my back as she listened to my heart and my breathing. She peeked into my ears. She made eye contact with me. Widowhood is lonely, and I was vibrating with the excitement of being touched by an adult human being. The doctor asked me about my child, and his father, and when I said, "he died of brain cancer six months ago," she stopped. That was how she knew me. She'd read Aaron's obituary. "How are you?" she asked me. Not in a small talk way, but in a doctor way.

I gave her the same answer I'd been giving everyone.

"Fine," I said, shrugging and playing with the ties of my paper gown, "you know, pretty good . . ."

She didn't know.

"Fine?" she said, skeptically. "Really? What are you doing to take care of yourself?"

I blinked. Take care of myself? I mean, lots! I was . . . well, I had bought myself a lot of things with money I didn't have. I let myself stay up super late watching whatever I wanted to watch. I let myself eat whatever I wanted. I meditated . . . sometimes. I was getting a tattoo removed. Those things counted, right?

She reached into her desk drawer and removed what looked like a worksheet.

"Okay, I'm just going to ask you a few questions . . ."

MY FRIEND TYLER HAS ALWAYS given me the advice I don't want to hear. Tyler and I met at a show in Brooklyn in 2006, where I was seeing a band he managed. We spent the entire night talking, giving each other crap, and deciding that we were going to be friends forever. It was basically a romantic comedy meet cute, but without the romance. A romance would have been impossible, because we are the same person, in different bodies, and nobody, even the biggest narcissist you know, wants to date themselves. Ten years later, it looks like we were right. Our friendship has lasted longer than a lot of marriages, even though our relationship has been entirely long distance. Tyler has always lived in Los Angeles, and I now live in Minneapolis. We have spent maybe three full days together over the course of a decade, but we've exchanged countless emails, chats, and text messages about everything from dating to daddy issues. Tyler can be brash and abrasive, but is also deeply introspective, empathic, and self-aware. At his worst, I have wanted to punch him in the face or push him off a cliff. At his best, he has been one of my greatest comforts. Admittedly, Tyler and I have the same worst qualities (judgmental, quick to anger, impulsive), and the same redeeming ones (deeply loyal and empathetic, very sentimental), but not always in equal measure, or at the same time. We can be mirrors for one another in ways that we can't be for ourselves. Which means that when Tyler tells me something I don't want to hear, I know I should listen. Tyler was right about every boyfriend he said was a waste of my time and my heart. I was right about every one of his vapid, awful girlfriends and each of the equally awful women he pined for. I was right when he met his now-wife, who was the opposite of every person he ever dated. Tyler was right when he told me I was falling in love with Aaron, but was too shy to say it myself.

"For fuck's sake, Nora," he nearly shouted at me over the phone, "say it! It will change your life. It changed mine."

Tyler, a relentless bachelor who was constantly pursuing a new beautiful, enigmatic creature, had recently dropped the L-word to a beautiful, kind woman who was refreshingly not trying to rip his heart from his chest. I had never heard him so happy, so settled, so domestic. The boy who never thought about marriage was thinking about proposing.

That night, lying in bed with Aaron, I stuttered that I had something to tell him. He looked at me as if I were about to reveal a third nipple and laughed out loud when I told him I loved him.

"I love you, too, dummy."

I called Tyler the night that Aaron was diagnosed with a brain tumor. Everyone around me was telling me how okay it was going to be, how the brain tumor wouldn't be cancerous, and life would go on as planned. Not Tyler.

"It's going to be bad, Nora. Whatever it is, it will be bad. And it will change your life. So, I just need you to brace yourself for it." Tyler waited patiently on the phone while I found an empty conference room in the hospital and shut myself inside. He was still on the line after I'd screamed out loud and knocked over several chairs. "I love you," he said, "you can do this."

After Aaron's death, friends were either extremely gentle with me, or extremely absent. Tyler was as close as he could be from a time zone away, and 0.0 percent gentle with me.

"Are you in therapy yet?" he'd text me.

Every. Single. Day.

The answer was always no. I wasn't in therapy. I didn't need therapy! I was FINE. Sure, I'd lost a pregnancy and a parent and a spouse within six weeks of each other. Yes, I'd spent three years caring for my husband and was now a widowed mother. Absolutely, those were sad things that happened to me. But could therapy cure sadness?

I listed out the things I did for myself: manicures, massages, meditating with the Oprah app! I ate organic. I exercised every day!

"You're an idiot." He'd reply.

Every. Single. Time.

I hated the word *caregiver*. I wasn't a caregiver. I was a wife. I was living my vows, down to the letter. In sickness and health, 'til death do us part. For three years, I made sure that Aaron took his chemo pills on time, made it to radiation, had all the red Gatorade he could drink until his taste buds changed and all he wanted was Lemonade Vitamin Water. I woke up thinking of Aaron, I fell asleep listening to the beat of his irregular heart. I've never eaten lobster because it freaks me out to think about breaking an exoskeleton to get to some weird, puffy meat that needs to be soaked in butter in order to seem appetizing, but I've often heard an anecdote about cooking them. If you drop a lobster in a pot of boiling water, they're acutely aware of their suffering. They scream. They panic. But place a lobster in a pot of cool water and raise the temperature slowly, and they don't even realize they're being boiled to death.

I was the second kind of lobster. And the first kind.

Aaron's brain cancer diagnosis was like being thrown into a pot of boiling water. We struggled and thrashed and tried our best to get out of it. But somewhere over the next three years, we just got used to it. A rolling boil of stress was my normal. It was comfortable to me. I couldn't even feel it.

But Tyler could.

"You're not okay," he'd say to me, "there's no way you're okay."

I bristled. Of course I was okay. I said I was okay! I was so okay that I was writing a book! And I had built a pretty good freelance career out of nothing! I was so good that I was not sleeping, like ever. Sometimes, if I were talking to a healthy man who was anywhere near my father or Aaron's age, I would watch their healthy faces fade into wan, dead faces while we were sitting together in a conference room. See? I was FINE!

"I have to tell you something and I don't want to be interrupted," he said when I picked up the phone one night. Before I could interrupt, he laid it out for me. "You need to see somebody. You need to go to therapy. Your fucking husband just died. Your dad died. You lost a pregnancy. Quit being a fucking idiot."

With that, the phone call was over.

Tyler was the first person I called after my doctor's appointment. "I'm seeing someone this week," I told him.

His naturally irritated voice softened. "Good," he said. "I love you, idiot."

I'd sent my therapist some reading materials in advance. A link to my blog, the obituary Aaron and I had written together, and related news articles. It seemed fair to give her a head start, a sense of what she was up against. She made me a cup of tea and showed me into her office, which was warm and worn, with an overstuffed couch that I naturally curled up into, kicking off my shoes and crossing my legs.

"So," she said. "You've had quite a year."

I opened my mouth to agree with her, but I was already crying.

An hour later, I was back in my car, calling Tyler.

"I'm in therapy," I told him. "You were right."

"No shit I was right!" he barked into the phone. I caught a glimpse of myself in the rearview mirror: puffy-faced, red-eyed, greasy-haired. I looked like I felt: like total hell, and the best I'd been in months.

Chapter Three

Don't Should Yourself

My friend Hans, who also likes to be identified as the senior producer of our podcast, *Terrible, Thanks for Asking*, visits his grandmother in the nursing home once a week. I'm telling you this because he would never want to brag about what a solidly good person he is, so I have to do it for him. And I'm telling you because I've been the beneficiary of Hans's good-hearted visits to his aging grandmother.

I hate the way we stereotype old people as "cute" or "wise." Old people are just people who have been on this earth for a long time, and calling them cute is demeaning, like they are human accessories, which they are not. *Babies* are cute little human accessories that we dress up. Old people *are* usually wise though, because you don't get through multiple decades on this earth without learning a thing or two, and you don't reach your seventies unless you've been dosed with a healthy spoonful or two of Not Giving A Crap Anymore. The older the person, the more likely I am to trust their opinions,* because they are so often no longer burdened by social norms or even basic manners. My mom is only sixty-seven, and she's already very comfortable telling me "how it is," especially when "how it is" is that my hair looked better long, or that my sweater looks like I got it at a thrift store but not in a good way.

One Sunday, Hans was visiting with Grandma and mentioned his friend Nora. I wasn't there for the conversation, but I assume it went something like this:

"Nora's great," he probably said, "she's just the best. Oh, and like you, her husband is also dead!" Grandma thought for a while, probably about how great I sounded, and gave Hans this advice to give to me. "You tell her this: don't should yourself. And don't let anyone should on you, either."

Hans's grandma. How did you know that we all needed this urgent message tattooed into our brains? Because you are WISE, that's how.

I am a master of should. I have always had the gift of knowing what other people should do, and the charming habit of either giving them my unsolicited point of view or being irrationally upset with them for not living up to my unspoken expectations. I have should all over people my entire life, but especially on myself. My obsession with my shoulds had me living my life as if it were a shared Google doc. I was paralyzed by the idea of what I *should* do, always turning to friends, family, and complete strangers at the nail salon who look like they have it together to see what *they* thought about my potential next steps in life. My own opinion has often come last, or not at all. I went to college right after high school not because I had

---

* Opinions on things that aren't related to politics, apologies to my many beloved elderly family members who I blocked on Facebook during the 2016 election.

a plan, or a passion to pursue, but because I thought I should go. I arrived at that expensive school directionless, and left the same way, probably because I spent those four years becoming the person that other people thought I should be. Freshman year: preppy Abercrombie model. Sophomore year: Paris Hilton party girl. Junior year: serious student who will start smoking because a boy she likes is a smoker. Senior year: wannabe grown-up who owns a closet full of "professional" clothing from Express. I then spent five years in New York, a city I didn't love, because, duh! You should love New York! I stayed with boyfriends I was incompatible with because I thought I should have a boyfriend. I accepted jobs that I should have wanted and built an entire career I was never meant to have, and a life I never meant to live.

If should were a person, it would be that friend of a friend who always talks over you at parties. If it were a software, it'd be a PowerPoint that advances automatically, or a locked pdf document that you can't fill out until you pay to update the software. That's comforting in some ways. Should offers you a direction to take and eliminates the stress of having to make any decisions yourself. But that clear direction has a price: it eliminates possibility and wonder from your life. There is no room for want or drive or your own humanity when should arrives, because should already has a plan.

Should happens (sorry). And when your life falls apart, should happens even more. When my husband Aaron died, should was everywhere I went. I was being should on by family, friends, and strangers on the internet who had access to a keyboard, an opinion, and a few scant facts about my life.

"You should refrain from making any decisions for at least a year," said people who didn't realize that not making any decisions is

1. a decision and

2. impossible when you're the only parent to a small child relying on you to make decisions like where he'll go to preschool, or where you'll live together. Children quite rudely insist on growing and changing exponentially each year. Kids will not pause for grief, even if you ask them nicely.

Besides, when you've spent years making *actual life-and-death decisions* for the person you love, any other decision is a vacation. Whether or not you sell a car or a house is nothing compared to deciding whether or not to continue chemo, or to pursue alternate therapies.

"You should move out of that house," said people who didn't realize that our house was haunted by Aaron, and that I still needed his ghost. I could see him out of the corner of my eye so often I could sometimes forget that he had died. I could tell myself, sitting in the basement and watching TV, that he'd just gone upstairs for a moment. Maybe to grab me a sparkling water or some snacks. I kept his spot open on the couch.

"You should stay in the house," said people who didn't realize that on the flip side, when Aaron's loss hit me, I wanted to light a match and burn the entire place to the ground. Some nights, walking into our empty bedroom was so difficult that I'd fall asleep on the couch, or in Ralph's Big Boy Bed, a twin from IKEA I'd dubiously assembled for him. Our house had been where we lived, and where Aaron died. It was the set for our major life scenes, and my brain would revisit them without my consent. Often and painfully.

"You should go back to work to get your mind off things," said people who thought my beloved dead husband was just an unpleasant thought I could banish to the back of my mind with mindless corporate busyness. There are not enough PowerPoints in the world to distract you from this kind of loss, and my body refused to keep a schedule that would be compatible with any desk job. I was often up all night long. I rearranged our kitchen cupboards at three a.m., started movies at midnight. Read through the most mundane of Aaron's emails, just trying to soak up any scraps of himself he had left behind.

"You should quit your job," said people who didn't know that Aaron and I had crawled deeply into debt over the course of his sickness. My career hadn't been a passion of mine, but it wasn't a hobby, either. It was a necessity. As crazy as this sounds, neither my mortgage lender nor my credit card issuer had realized that for me, Earth had stopped rotating on November 25, 2014. Both of those wacky entities still wanted me to pay my bills. On time. With *money*.

The people who were quick to offer me a comforting should were people who had never been in my position. They had living husbands to help them raise their children, dads they could turn to for advice. Partners who helped them with a second income. They were on their second healthy pregnancy, ready to deliver at any moment. Their lives were unfolding in the way they had expected, and mine had not. My discomfort made them uncomfortable. I was a living, breathing, publicly crying reminder that their own lives could go off the rails at any time. What happened to us deviated from should and rejected the natural order of things. Truly, a father shouldn't die at age thirty-five from a horrible cancer. His wife shouldn't have a miscarriage right before then. That's not something that should happen! These shoulds that were so kindly offered to me assumed that chaos can be managed, that every problem has an answer, that tragedy can be managed if you just follow The Plan of the Should. The people offering me these shoulds were trying to provide comfort. Not just for me, but for themselves. If I could be fixed, if I could be okay again, get back into the natural order of things, then their comfortable lives didn't feel so precarious.

After Aaron's death I developed a bad habit of starting any book I was reading by flipping to the last page. Out of context that page made no sense, but as the story progressed, remembering those last three hundred words or so made me feel safe. This was all going somewhere. It would be resolved. All I wanted was to be able to flip to the last page of this part of my life, and know that whatever I chose to do next, things would turn out all right. That's not the way books are intended to be read, and it's not the way life can be lived. I could have followed any of those shoulds, or none of those shoulds, and the result would have been the same. I'd still have the same gaping hole in the middle of my soul. Aaron would still be dead. I would still have to live my life without him.

That meant that every piece of advice, every should, was worthless. Because of all the people offering me some navigational assistance, none of them could actually do these things for me. The only person responsible for my life—the only person who could and would live it—was me. No matter what kind of Steering Committee formed around me, I had to do the work.

Personal responsibility is such a bummer.

Without Aaron, I'd fallen back into being the kind of girl I'd been before I knew him, consumed by what I should do, with what was expected of me. Some friends of Aaron's come for dinner and I feel like the sad orangutan at the free zoo in Saint Paul. I can never stand to stop in front of the enclosure, and watch how bewildered she seems by all of the attention. How the hell should she know how an orangutan should act? She lives in a zoo!

It's a painfully silent dinner and I feel their eyes on me constantly, searching. They do not know what they are looking for, and neither do I. They are just here to observe me, to see a wild widow up close, to say they were here.

I get the sense that they are disappointed in the visit. That I am neither sad enough nor happy enough. I do not meet their expectations.

I want desperately to please everyone, to show them whatever version of me they are seeking. Which Nora would you like to see today? Sad Nora? Inspirational Nora? Numb Nora?

Plenty of people told me that I should give my child stability and routine, but I knew that the thing Ralph needed more than a schedule was a mom who wasn't just going through the motions. Children, like the very elderly, are not beholden to the law of should. When Ralph needed to cry, he cried. When he was angry, he screamed. I didn't love that second one when I was trying to buckle him into a car seat in a crowded parking lot, but I had to respect it. He wasn't hiding anything. Somewhere between our youngest years and our oldest years we learn to hide behind Shoulds and Woulds and Coulds, instead of feeling and facing what Is.

What is . . . is this: I am a young widow who has fallen in love again. I am pregnant with this new love's baby. The shoulds in this version of my life are compounding quickly with all of these facts. And these facts are good. Love is good. Kids are good. Life is good. But should it be?

I am a widow, so I should be sad and depressed. I am also a published author who met Jennifer Weiner at a party and whose first book was read by Mandy Moore, so I should be very happy and grateful. I am in love again, with a man who has two fantastic children of his own, children who have fully embraced Ralph and me as a part of their lives. I should be doubly grateful for that. Triple, quadruple grateful. I should not be on antidepressants and having panic attacks in my car! I should be showing off beautiful Phoenix feathers, preening publicly about my rise from the ashes. I should be the poster child for what it means to move on, to get over it, to live your best life!

I am happy. And I'm really, really fucking sad.

I don't need to worry about anyone else shoulding on me. I'm shoulding all over myself.

Chapter Four

I Can't Even

You don't realize how fast and loose people play with meaningful words like "single parent" until the words mean something to you. "I'm a single parent this week," women in my barre class would sigh, "my husband is traveling for work." I would wrap my thighs tighter around the blue ball between my legs and try to crush it with my contempt. People will say this on Facebook, on their Instagram stories, or in hurried conversations at the grocery store, asserting their aloneness in a pursuit in which some people are *actually, truly alone.* I felt, after Aaron died, a burning defensiveness not only for myself, but for truly single parents. Not middle-class wives whose husbands would undoubtedly return home Friday evening for a family night of Chinese takeout and a movie, men who were just a FaceTime away from any unruly children. Not wealthy people with nannies to help with errands and childcare. Not average divorced people who alternated weeks or days with their children. All of these people had an out—a potential break from the tyranny of childrearing, somewhere on the horizon. Truly, truly single parents do not. There is no partner returning on a set day or time, nobody to text when your child is driving you bonkers or reaches a milestone.

It is just you.

Pointing out this reality is not something you are allowed to do, or even think about. As mothers, we're required by an unspoken code to unconditionally support one another. We accept the choices that other mothers make without judgment, we acknowledge that all our experiences and feelings are valid and wish each other well on our individual journeys.

LOL, yeah right.

I am fully aware that these thoughts are uncharitable. I don't know what it's like to be divorced, or to have a terrible husband, or to feel abandoned in my marriage. Or to even have a husband away on business. The only thing I know is my own experience, and part of every lived experience is a natural amount of judgment and envy, two feelings that are amplified by the difficulties of motherhood. We all want to know that we are doing a good enough job for the small human beings that have been placed in our care, and we are all sure that someone else has it better or is doing a better job.

One day, in that same barre class, as we did our check-ins and tucked our tails and carved our thighs, I got the full-on dose of perspective I didn't know I needed. I was squeezing my inflatable ball between my legs, channeling the anger I was feeling that day into a rounder butt, halfheartedly listening to the women around me describe their perfect lives. And then, she spoke. A woman I'd quietly envied—hated, but just a little—for her perfection. She wasn't talking, she was sobbing. Everything was falling apart and had been for a long time. This class was the only thing she had to look forward to today, or any day. "I'm sorry," she laughed to herself, wiping her nose on her sweat towel and folding herself back into the version of herself that acted like everything was fine. She offered no further details, and nobody seemed to need them. It was clear by the silence in the room, that we were all starring in the same exact play, just with our own artistic interpretation. We were all doing a great job of pretending that we were fine.

"I'm sorry," I said out loud, to her, and to everyone else.

The stomach flu hit me hard the winter after Aaron died. I put Ralph to bed early, and spent the night in the bathroom, sweating and shivering on the floor between puke sessions. I woke up on the tile floor to the sound of Ralph crying. Even at his sickest, Aaron would have been awake to take his turn on parental duty given my sorry state. But Aaron was dead, and I had nobody to cry out for. "I'm coming, buddy!" I called to Ralphie, and tried to stand. I was too weak and too nauseous to balance on two feet, so I crawled to his bedroom. When he stopped crying, I laid on the floor next to his bed like a dog.

I was alone, but I hadn't always been alone. For that reason, single parenthood felt like a badge I wasn't qualified to wear. Solo Parent, which seemed snappier, seemed to have been claimed by those temporarily abandoned by business travel. What was I, besides a sweaty mother with bad puke breath, laying on her son's bedroom floor, weeping for the man we'd both lost?

"We're *widowed* moms," Moe told me over and over, "we're not normal people anymore." Moe looks exactly like eighties Jon Bon Jovi: big, curly hair; cut-up T-shirts; tight jeans; big smile. We met in the winter, just after we'd each been widowed. I was just two months out from Aaron's death. Moe's husband, Andy, had died by suicide just a few months before Aaron. Loss is what brought us together, and love is what has kept us together. We became each other's Person: the one to text about our fatherless boys, the one to call in the middle of the night when it felt like the whole world's sadness was piled on my chest. All of the things I didn't know how to say, Moe already understood. She knew in the first two seconds of a phone call whether I was calling to laugh, to scream, or to sob uncontrollably. Moe knew what it was like to remember without trying: three chords from an old song brought Andy back to her, lanky and young, dancing in their living room. Moe is a naturally independent person. She can catch and clean her own fish, even though she's so allergic she has to do so while wearing rubber surgical gloves. She changes her own oil. When something is broken, Moe can fix it herself. If she or Andy got a flat tire, Moe stepped right up. But Moe preferred doing things with Andy. She liked that he made balanced dinners—a carb, a protein, a vegetable—every night, even though her gluten-free, dairy-free, vegetarian diet made that simple task infinitely more complicated. She liked raising Bronson with Andy, and how they'd established their own little family traditions: morning dances in the kitchen, nightly parades through the house with their dog and cat trailing behind them as they each played an instrument. Moe could do it all on her own, she just didn't want to.

I'd removed Aaron's brain surgery staples and I'd pushed a human being out of my body, but I don't have Moe's natural strength and independence. The first time I watched TV after Aaron died, I sat in the basement screaming and crying because there were three remote controls, and I didn't know what any of them actually controlled. That winter, I sat in the parking lot of a gas station, consulting my car's manual to learn how to pop the hood and pour in some windshield washer fluid. I'd signed up to do things alone; I didn't think I could do them.

I bristled at the admiration people poured my way. "You're so strong!" "I don't know how you do it!" Didn't they know how hard it was realizing that you were the only one who could remember to pick up milk on the way home? The only one who could pick up your son when he cried? Even if you were sick. The only person who could shovel the sidewalk when the sky dropped six inches of snow and the wind chill was minus eleven degrees Fahrenheit? Of course, they didn't know. I didn't know any of that, back when Aaron and I had decided to start this family. Not really.

"You'll have to do this alone someday," he whispered to me one night.

"I can do it," I said, kissing his tears away, not realizing I was lying to his face.

I was worried about everything as a widowed mom, because I had no one to discuss anything with. I had no one to tell me I was overreacting, overthinking, no one to do the parts I couldn't handle. Ralph's lymph nodes were swollen . . . did he have cancer? Did you see the way his eye sort of drifts in photos? Is he on the spectrum? He doesn't know how to throw or catch a ball . . . how am I supposed to teach him things I don't give a crap about? Is he going to be the weird kid in school who lives with his weird mom who never taught him how to throw a ball? I once had a friend tell me that just the act of buying a parenting book proves that you are a good parent. She was probably just trying to make me feel better, but I hold on to that thought during the first months of widowed parenthood, when everything is harder than it should be, and all my parenting books sit unopened on my bedside table.

When everything feels hard, small victories feel like huge ones. As a surprise, I bought Ralph a tricycle with an additional steering handle sprouting up from the back. The handle lets a parent steer their kid along, without having to hunch over and push them like a stalled car. It was genius, except that it arrived at my door unassembled. The toolbox was in the garage, and I was aware, suddenly, that Aaron had been the last person to touch this box, and everything inside it. Aaron would know how to assemble this tricycle without the instructions, but I need to read them several times before I can even begin the assembly process. It's easier than I think it will be, and when it's finished, I call Ralph into the room to see his new ride. "Look, buddy!" I shout and pick the trike up by the handlebars . . . which completely come free from the rest of the bike, as it goes crashing to the living room floor. "Is it broken?" Ralph asks, while I momentarily consider throwing the entire thing through the picture window. Later that day, Ralph and I take his trike for its maiden voyage. He is not great at steering, and the grown-up steering handle helps me keep him from jumping the curb and hitting a parked car. He doesn't understand this, and he resents it. He's two and a half, after all. "Let go!" He demands of me, periodically turning his head—and the entire bike with it. I refuse, and we are immediately that family, having a loud altercation on an otherwise quiet street. Ralph narrows his eyes at me and screams. "I. CAN. DO IT!"

Well, then. That makes one of us.

Solo parent, single parent, widowed parent.

However it is you're doing this parenting thing . . . you're doing it.

Chapter Five

Arranged

I was on the hunt for a love affair. Okay, not a love affair, but an affair. And maybe not an affair, but some sort of sexual experience that sounded more respectable that just banging some random guy. Please pardon my self slut-shaming, I was raised Catholic.

I had been widowed six months earlier, at thirty-one. And while my heart had withered and died alongside my husband Aaron, my body remained alive and that rolling boil of grief inside of me was matched with an equal amount of lust. This was an indiscriminate lust. Not just of the sexual variety (though, yeah, that for sure) but just the appreciation of the living human body in almost all of its adult forms. I would find myself, in public, thoroughly undone at the site of a strange man's forearm while he read the paper, at the shoulders of the male person in front of me at yoga. All around me were beautiful, walking miracles and I wanted—no, I needed—to be naked with one. I felt so guilty about this. My husband had just died. How could I be feeling this? But aside from anger, the only thing I could feel was palpable desire. That real deep and gut-wrenching grief that I felt deep inside of me was too hot to touch just yet, but the desire was right at the surface. I had three modes: Blistering Anger, Complete Detachment, and Fantasizing About the Man in Front of Me at the Grocery Store. Detachment was not a form of Zen, but a form of emotional stagnation I'd been dropped into. One where I could recite my life script as if I were talking about a complete stranger:

"Hi, I'm Nora. I was widowed six months ago right after I lost a pregnancy and my dad died. So, do you live around here?"

I knew that some very sad things had happened—I was sad about them, I swear!—but I couldn't access that sadness. I didn't have the security clearance for it yet. I was removed from the world, and from myself. Feeling desire was at least feeling something, and I wanted to feel. Specifically, I wanted to feel some hands on me that didn't belong to my toddler son.

But, like, how? Earlier in my life, this had not been hard to accomplish. I wanted the freedom of my early twenties back, but it's hard to capture when you're a mother and you are concerned about how you'll provide for your child, and everyone around you has grown up and is no longer interested in just rolling around together for a little while. What I wanted and couldn't find in my twenties—to be paired off—was now what everyone wanted, or already had. I'd somehow passed beyond the age or lifestyle for a casual sexual encounter, which left dating as the only option. This was . . . not ideal. I didn't want to date. I didn't want to have dinner or pretend to care about someone's life story. I didn't want to explain myself to anyone, because that would have meant revising my script to say, "I am a recent widow who wants nothing from you except your naked body on top of mine." I had tried to do the swipey-app stuff, with no success. I live in Minneapolis, which is a big enough city until you are trying to troll for a no-strings-attached hookup on the internet and find yourself matched with the big brother of one of your childhood friends. What the heck did a widow have to do to have some no-strings-attached—yet respectful and safe—intercourse with a stranger?

I met him at my sister's dance show. My sister is nine years older than me. She is also a white woman. She is also a Bollywood enthusiast who became an active member of Minnesota's largest (only?) Bollywood dance troupe. They had sold out several nights of their show in a sizable theater, and I watched in awe of her, onstage in a swirl of color and movement. Backstage after the show, there he was dressed in a white undershirt, the only man there taller than my six feet. "Nice job," I said, "we should make out sometime." He looked at me with shock and then said, "Yes, we should!" My sister took it from there, like any wingwoman would. "She's serious," she told him after I left, "she's coming to the after-party and you should *totally* make out with her."

He was perfect in every way: tall, handsome, and unavailable. He was engaged, which may make you hate me. But he hadn't even met his fiancée, so it felt like a little bit of a gray area that maybe we could work around? Okay, look, none of this was good. Except it was. It was so good. It was so good to have warm hands on me that didn't belong to a child. It felt so good to have a secret. To have a person tell me that I was beautiful, desirable. The situation had all the makings of a great rom-com: both of us were unavailable, we had established at the outset that neither of us were allowed to develop feelings for the other, both of us understood that this was an unviable romantic relationship with limitless physical possibilities . . . both of us were certain that with this understanding, nothing could possibly go wrong.

What could go wrong and did go wrong is that people have feelings, even (especially) when they agree not to have them. That is the obvious plotline of every rom-com!

One night I woke at three a.m., having accidentally fallen asleep. He was sleeping beside me, and for a few gorgeous moments, I thought he was Aaron. The realization was too much, and I gathered my things in the dark, rushed to my car, and wept my apologies to my dead husband.

Still, I went back to his small apartment a few nights later. His sweet smile and his kind eyes sometimes made me forget that this was just pretend, that he was just a person whose bed I snuck into after my son had gone to sleep and my mother had agreed to "baby-sit" while I went somewhere that was *none of her business and would you please stop asking.*

We had both agreed this was nothing, but I was not the only person who was forgetting that. He would wonder aloud how Ralph would react to him, and I would remind him that he would never meet Ralph. He would wonder if his parents would disown him should he cancel his arranged marriage, and I would remind him that I was not a suitable replacement for any fiancée, for many reasons. He spoke to his family every day, sometimes while I was there, and his language was like a song. Sometimes he would speak it to me as he played with my hair. He could have very easily just been reciting his Target list, but it lulled me into a peaceful place where my imagination could run wild.

This was the affair I needed—that we both needed—a sweet, kind distraction from the realities of our lives: that I was an unlovable pariah and that he would be the good son and make his parents proud with the suitable woman they'd selected for him. A suitable woman who was certainly not a widowed mother.

In a few months, I knew, his fiancée would arrive and this would end. He would get married, buy a house, and have his own babies. I would use these moments with him, and then the memories of him, to fight off the loneliness as long as I could, before moving on to another emotionally unavailable man. It was the perfect solution! One emotionally unavailable magnet attracting another, one empty affair after another to chase away and protect my loneliness for years to come.

He was fascinated by what he saw as my freedom—I could choose who I wanted to be with and do what I wanted with my life. I thought he was insane. Didn't he know that I was a widow, and a mother? That it was unlikely that men would be lining up to take on all of my emotional excess? The idea of a completely blank page of a future didn't seem like freedom, it seemed like a trap. Where was I supposed to go from here? I was fascinated by the rigidity of his life, and a tiny bit jealous of it, too. Everything for him was so certain. He'd picked his career at age sixteen and followed the path diligently, even when it led him to the frozen tundra of Minnesota, far from his family. Now, his parents had selected his life partner. All he had to do was stop having sex with me and show up at the airport when his future arrived.

This affair made me even more deeply protective over my relationship with Aaron. Nobody could know that I was sleeping with someone else, because nobody would understand it. Well, nobody but Moe. "Good for you!" she said. "You need this. And you're allowed it." But was I? Was I actually allowed, six months after Aaron's death, to be sneaking around the city with a man who was engaged to someone else, and if so, could I get that in writing?

Reminders of Aaron kept showing up, little signs that he was still with me, still looking out for me. Obscure songs from our courtship played on the radio when I started my car. I would always happen to look at the clock at either 8:21—his birth date, August 21—or at 11:25—his death date. A cardinal started sitting outside my bedroom window. Look, it doesn't sound like much, but trust me, this was all Aaron. An email from Ticketmaster arrived, and for some reason I didn't mark it as spam. It was the tickets Aaron had bought for us to Taylor Swift's 1989 Tour, one of the last things he did on his deathbed. Let me repeat and clarify that: on his deathbed, my thirty-five-year-old husband used his mother's American Express to purchase the first release of Taylor Swift tickets for a concert that would take place ten months after his eventual death. The tickets arrived, and they were very, very good tickets (thanks, Kimmer!). Taylor was a huge part of my relationship with Aaron. When we met in 2010, Aaron already believed her to be the pop icon she would eventually become. He was the only adult man I knew who had an opinion on Taylor Swift. And his opinion was that he loved her deeply, and someday the world would, too. Her *Red* album was the soundtrack to his first brain surgery and our first year of marriage, a physical CD we purchased at Target just to make sure we got the bonus tracks. I am not embarrassed by any of this, because I think pop music is a true art form, and that the artistic merit of any song is measured by how it echoes through the experiences of your life.

My big sister Meghan was the only person I could imagine taking Aaron's place at this show, and I felt Aaron's approval when she accepted my offer. But days before the show, more tickets arrived. Had Aaron, in the end stages of brain cancer, bought tickets twice? Twice before in our relationship we'd surprised each other with tickets to the same show . . . had I done that and forgotten? No. And No. These were tickets from someone else. From my affair. He knew I was going with my sister, he said, but maybe he could go, too? Or my sister could bring her husband, and we could all go together? No. And No. AND NO!!!

All of the illusions I'd let myself believe in dissolved in an instant. The desire was gone, and the rage was back. The spell was broken, and so was everything else. The small space I'd made for this man in my heart collapsed. He was done. We were done. No. I said, this is not something that *we* do. This is something I did with Aaron. With my dead husband. Not with you, not with anyone else.

I was not kind and I was not gracious. I was angry. I was angry that I had tricked myself into believing that there was a substitute for grief, and that it was this . . . mess. I was not a carefree twenty-something. I was a deeply wounded thirty-something mother. He was engaged.

I deleted his number, but he called me anyway. He called me over and over and over, and I finally answered. He wanted me to know it was over. I was relieved—he got it—our fling, our tidy little entanglement that was just about sex, was over. But I'd misunderstood. He didn't mean we were over—he meant his *engagement* was over.

"Why did you do this?!" I shouted, as quietly as I could without waking my child, who was sleeping next to me in bed.

He had thrown away that perfectly planned-out life for a person he'd known for a few weeks, someone so broken she hadn't even really started grieving for the life she'd lost yet. He loved me. And he would wait for me. He had made a huge mistake. But he didn't see it this way. Even when his parents told his brother, who called him, panicked, urging him to get it together, to tell their parents he had not been in his right mind when he called to tell them he was throwing away the future they'd planned for him to take a chance on a recently widowed white lady with a toddler, he didn't think he was making a mistake. Not even when he found out that the answer to the hypothetical "Will my family disown me if I back out of an arranged marriage?" was an absolutely real "YEP!" Not when the daily phone calls from home stopped. Not when he found himself alone in a foreign country, his family so deeply ashamed of his Westernization they refused to speak to him.

He stuttered as he relayed all of this to me, slowly realizing the gravity of what he had done as he heard the words out loud. He thought . . . he thought things were different from what we agreed they were. He wanted me to be happy about his choice, he had expected me to show up on his doorstep and replace the fiancée I'd helped him betray, to combine my chaotic world with his orderly one and create something and new. He'd wait, he said. Ten years? Fifteen? As long as it took.

There was no point in waiting for me. It really wasn't him; it was me. He was beautiful and kind and wholehearted. I was broken and dead inside. I wasn't worth planning a life around or throwing a life plan away for. I didn't know what I was doing or where I was going. Five minutes or five years, I wasn't worth the wait.

His carefully curated life was now as broken as mine, and why? Because when my mouth said "don't love me" my actions had screamed "love me love me love me!" I texted him in the middle of the day, just to see how he was doing. I held his hand when he drove. I replied to his "good morning" texts. And I knew that I shouldn't, I knew that my "don't love me" disclaimer didn't speak louder than any of those actions. Maybe a small part of me was hoping that just a few months after Aaron died, this unlikely romance would cure me. That against all odds, against all my protest, this would be real. I was playing pretend, lost in make-believe. What was the worst that could happen?

Well! Outside of my world of make-believe, there was a humiliated woman on the other side of the world wondering how and why her carefully planned life had fallen apart. There were two sets of parents exploding with shame and anger. And there was a sweet, kind man on the other side of my telephone who thought this phone call was going to go very, very differently. I hung up the phone and cried as quietly as I could. Because my broken heart had broken another heart, and a few more around that one. If a widow kisses an engaged man in Minnesota, how many hearts will shatter in Chennai, India?*

My sister insists that I am overblowing my role in the explosion of this man's life. She assures me that he was never that interested in an arranged marriage, that he always had reservations, and that I was just a very convenient, very beautiful (my words, not hers) escape hatch from that reality.

We were both playing make-believe, I guess. We were both lost and scared, looking for someone to cling to. It feels good to have that absolution, even secondhand. I have not spoken to him since. I have not looked at his Facebook profile or even looked through the photos of mutual friends to see if I can catch him in the background. Pinky swear, that's how emotionally mature I am. Or that's how avoidant I am.

My sister, though, reports that he is doing well. That he bought a townhouse, and a BMW, and that he met a very nice Indian girl here in Minnesota.

Maybe they'll even get married.

---

* The answer is between five and ten, possibly more. Do not do this.

Chapter Six

Baggage

It was clear that I was not prepared for the dating process. Though not many people are truly prepared for holding themselves up to the scrutiny of strangers over a meal or an activity, searching for common emotional and/or physical ground, hoping to find a needle of commitment in a haystack of hookups. My recent foray into homewrecking aside, I can admit that while I had certainly participated in the dating game before my marriage to Aaron, I had never been *great* at dating. I'd never be called up to an All-Star team. I was mostly a benchwarmer, probably because when I made it onto the court, I was bound to either get hurt or make someone hurt. Can you tell I don't watch a lot of sports, or are these metaphors working?

The first time a boy broke up with me, it broke me. This sounds dramatic, and it should, because I was sixteen years old.

It's over.

I go back and forth between wondering what I ever saw in him, and wondering if anyone will ever see anything in me.

I'd fallen in love with this boy the first day of high school. Which also sounds dramatic, but when you are fifteen and Eros hits you with a bolt of lightning during freshman orientation, you're powerless over your destiny. We dated for a year, and it was emotionally turbulent because *I* was emotionally turbulent and he was a sixteen-year-old boy with limited emotional capacity and I wanted to marry him and have a thousand of his babies and he said he loved me and doesn't that mean, like, forever? Your first love feels like it is destiny. It feels perfectly logical to kiss a boy on your parents' front steps and think, "I am done looking, I have kissed the last mouth I will ever kiss. I am going to marry this mouth and the boy it's attached to." It feels absolutely *right* to imagine what your kids will look like, and dream of a far-off day, when you're both old—twenty-two or twenty-three, maybe—and you can get married and have all the sex you want and really start your lives, you know? That plan felt perfectly logical—to me, at least. And I have the diary entries to prove it.

This boyfriend and I went to a teeny tiny high school together and if he didn't love me anymore, would anyone else love me, ever? Surely, now that I was marked as having belonged to him for an entire academic year, nobody else *could* ever love me. It was against the laws of the social contract, the laws of physics, probably even the legal laws. Once you've been loved by one person, how can another person in such close proximity feel the same way about you?

These are real thoughts and real concerns that were in my soft little head at the time, and when I revealed them to one of my closest friends, while we were in my room applying one of our thirty-seven layers of makeup before going to this ex-boyfriend's football game, she made eye contact with me in the mirror and looked at me like I'd just drop-kicked a baby seal. "NORA," Erin said between lip gloss applications, "I never want to hear you say that AGAIN." Erin had just broken up with her first boyfriend, who responded to this news by spending every bus ride to school sitting directly in front of us, blasting the Goo Goo Dolls and wiping tears from his eyes. In the weeks since their breakup, Erin had caught the eye of basically every other boy in our school because . . . of course she did! We were all just hormones wrapped in skin and school uniforms at that age! But it didn't feel that way. I felt like Joni Mitchell, who learned the truth at seventeen that love was made for beauty queens. Erin was the Prom Queen. She was undeniably beautiful, hilarious, and didn't give a crap what anyone thought of her. Of *course* someone would love her again. Of *course* she hadn't squandered her only chance at love by age sixteen. But I knew, on some level, that I had.

I *didn't* say it again, but I definitely thought it again. And again. And again. Well into my twenties, with every relationship that dissolved, I was sure that my capacity for love, and being loved, was somehow diminishing. It felt like romantic love was a finite resource, and that my capacity for having it in my life was sliding through my fingers with every unreturned text message, every second date that didn't materialize. The only measure for a successful relationship was that it lasted forever, so what did that make every relationship that had an expiration date? A big failure. A waste of time. A reassurance that I was for sure as unlovable as I thought I was at age sixteen.

Not only was my future disappearing, but my past was adding up. Each doomed relationship had the potential to become baggage, which as I understood it was extremely undesirable. To have baggage means that you have had relationship experiences that you bring forward with you. You know, things that have affected you, formed you, and not for the better. You don't want to have *baggage* when you go into a new relationship, you want to arrive with just the clothes on your back. Any past experiences are just that—in the past. You want to be a person with no past, the human equivalent of a goldfish, completely unencumbered by anything you'd ever seen and experienced, all of your history evaporating from your little goldfish brain, placing you blessedly and perpetually in the present moment.

Everyone puts their best foot forward in a dating profile, putting time into the selection of photos and the self-descriptions. You've got just a few sentences to snag the potential Love of Your Life while they swipe through a seemingly endless catalog of available humans. As my friend Faye designed her dating profile, she made a conscious decision to include her relationship status, which doesn't sound like anything daring, except that her relationship status was "Widow." She worried about that one single word and the effect it might have on potential mates. She feared that one word would disqualify her from the dating game. It might be "too much" for a man to know that she had loved someone before, had promised herself to be with him until death do they part. It might be a lot to take in that death, courtesy of a light-rail train in Minneapolis and an intersection he crossed every day, had parted Faye and her husband.

That's a fair concern to have, because it's a lot to live through when it happens to you. I shared the same concerns as Faye when I started dating. My husband had not died suddenly. Aaron had been treated for brain cancer for three years before he died, and I knew from revealing that information even in platonic situations that it had one of two effects on people: it could clam them up or open them like an automatic door.

But when you see enough people recoil in horror at the facts of your life, you start to feel that the only way to be worthy of love is to be footloose, fancy free, and devoid of any traces of trauma, grief, or even basic human emotions. Plenty of my widow friends have left that word off their dating profiles, have struggled with when and how to "reveal" this truth to a potential suitor. Plenty of my not-widowed friends have their own things that they're sure would be "too much" for someone to possibly opt in to loving them. None of those things involve incinerating somebody you once shared a bed with.

The night they first met, Faye's date asked about her first husband. He asked about her experience as a widow. About what her first marriage was like. Why, he wondered, would she think he'd be deterred by her loss? Doesn't *everyone* experience loss? Why would it scare him that she'd been loved, that she'd had a healthy relationship? Shouldn't everyone have that in life? Why would we categorize our universal human experiences of loss, love, and grief as something negative?

Faye married this guy, because *duh*.

Unless you marry the person you met at age fifteen at high school orientation when you were shiny and new, everyone you meet will come to you in some other-than-new state: pre-owned, slightly used, refurbished. No matter how slick and shiny we look on the outside, we've all got some miles on us. And that's not a bad thing. After Aaron's death, I found myself gravitating toward people who wore their miles proudly, who showed up with whatever they were carrying and just laid it out there. Not polite people, or perfect people. Just . . . people. The kind who tell you the truth when you ask how they are, who don't even think about lying and telling you that everything is fine. It's not like I was trolling Craigslist for Damaged Humans, but something inside me started to pull me toward people who had also experienced hard things. I lost my taste for fiction and devoured memoirs, soaking up the experiences of people who lived and felt deeply. I made friends with people who had gone through their own stuff and I realized that, romantically, I needed someone who had been through some shit, too. Someone who had been to the dark places, who had walked through the fire. Someone who had suffered at the hands of love, and who was willing to do it again.

I am proud to be a widow. I am proud to have loved someone so much. I am proud to say I am still here, that I am getting through it. I am proud of the love I shared with Aaron, and who it made me today. If this is baggage, it's at least the fancy Louis Vuitton stuff. But I don't think it's baggage. I don't think that Aaron—that loving him, losing him—is something I'm trying to jam into the overhead compartment when it clearly needs to be checked.

Even if they're often heavy and unwieldy, our past lives are not baggage. They are not defects; they are features. Our past experiences—especially the hard ones—help us navigate the world around us and ahead of us.

Aaron died at age thirty-five, and that will always be tragic and it will always make me sad. But our love and his death are not a burden to me, and will not be a burden to the person who loves me next. Aaron's love and Aaron's death are my foundation. They're my standard for love and marriage and strength and bravery. They are not a hurdle to overcome, they are the stable place I get to build from. This is what I know, what I've learned from life. I wish I could tell my teenage self that loving once makes you better at loving, and better at being loved. That whatever happens with each love, you can carry it all proudly.

"WIDOWED MOM SEEKS HUMAN MALE WHO HAS BEEN THROUGH SOME SHIT"

What kind of shit? I don't know! You tell me. Tell me *everything*. Tell me about the worst thing that's happened to you, the darkest place you've been. Tell me what happened next, how you picked up the pieces—some of them, at least; they're not all worth keeping—and made something new. Tell me what happens next, where you're heading, and who you want by your side. Tell me what keeps you up at night, or if you sleep like an old dog (not like a baby, you should know that babies don't sleep that well).

About me: I'm very tall, very widowed. A mom to a toddler boy who has an Oedipal complex and thinks he's going to marry me (just want you to be aware of the competition you're up against). I'm opinionated, obstinate, and obsessive. I am quick to anger, quick to cry, quick-witted and a slow runner. A very slow runner. I don't know if you can really call it running, really. I don't know what I want. Some heavy making out? Someone to text me for no reason? A person who is absolutely, positively in love with me? It varies, day by day. I know that I want you to play with my hair while we lay on the couch and listen to records. I want you to hold my hand while we're driving and take out the trash before you're ever asked. I want you to want me, but not need me. To be there for me without my asking, and to go away without being told. I want you to keep me company and keep your promises.

PS: Please, don't be shorter than me.

Chapter Seven

Finders Keepers

Like all the most cliché and annoying love stories and love songs, your smug coupled friends like to say "I found him when I wasn't looking." I didn't even really find him, if you want to know the even more cliché, more annoying truth. He was handed to me on a silver platter: a brand-new love, handpicked for me by my friend Moe, the cofounder of the Hot Young Widows Club and the only friend qualified to vet the next great love of my life.

It was fall. The same season when I'd met Aaron, and when I'd lost him. But fall includes a veritable laundry list of anniversaries tied to Aaron's love, sickness, and death. They are as follows:

OCTOBER 21, 2010: When I met Aaron

NOVEMBER 3, 2010: Our first date

NOVEMBER 3, 2011: Aaron's first brain surgery

NOVEMBER 30, 2011: Aaron's first day of radiation

DECEMBER 3, 2011: Our wedding

NOVEMBER 25, 2014: Aaron's death

DECEMBER 3, 2014: Aaron's funeral

I don't need any of these dates marked in my calendar to remember them—though they are listed in all my Google calendars anyway. Before these anniversaries show up as calendar reminders, my body remembers them. I'll wake up stiff and aching, my body bracing itself for what happened years ago on that day. Even if my brain were wiped clean, my muscles, my organs, and especially my heart would always remember. Even if I'd been kept in a locked room without access to a calendar, I'd have known that Aaron's deathaversary was growing near. Your mind can try its best to forget, to avoid, but the body remembers. As our son jumped in piles of leaves and the Minnesota air started to chill, I could feel myself growing harder. My shoulders found a resting place right next to my ears. I woke up with an aching jaw, having bitten holes into my retainer as I slept. My eyeballs pulsed in my head all day long, and my heart raced. My grief had so many layers that it had become an exoskeleton. It was a hard, crusty emotional shell that only I could see. It was ugly, but oddly comfortable, and I had pretty much planned on spending the rest of my life in it.

By early November, the dread had filled me completely, and was spilling out in very productive ways. For example, by spending the better part of a week inside, hunched over my computer, arguing with idiots on the internet. I was able to convincingly act as if this was indeed the best use of my time, and that it wasn't just a misdirected way of working through my inner emotional turmoil. My little brother, sensing that I may not be providing the most wonderful home environment for my toddler at that moment, invited Ralph to sleep over at his house up the street, leaving me alone with my thoughts and my rage and my laptop, giving me all the space I could need to dig into some online comments and educate Greg H. from Burnsville, Minnesota, on rape culture. I tucked in for a super-chill Saturday night.

Instead, my friend Moe asked me to come over and burn some things in her backyard, and because I never grew out of the pyro phase of my childhood, where my cousins and I would spend family gatherings around the votive tabletop candles, melting plastic forks into small sculptures, I said yes. And even though Moe has seen me at my worst both emotionally and physically, I put on mascara and changed into pants with a zipper. I drove to her house in Saint Paul, where the bonfire "party" she promised turned out to be me, Moe, and our friend Kevin sitting around a fire and drinking boxed wine. I was relieved. Parties are stressful and interacting with more than a few people at a time had become impossible for me since Aaron died. Aaron was always the life of the party, adept at navigating any social situation. I hung on to him like a barnacle. Without a very social whale to cling to, a barnacle is hard to bring to a party.

As far as a night out goes for me, it was great. I was out in public (sort of). I got to burn things, which, as I've previously noted, is something I enjoy. I didn't have to mess with a wine opener. And then, the back gate swung open and another person joined our party. He was dark-haired and beardy and wearing a hoodie underneath a nylon jacket, a combination that made him look like an adult toddler. I thought "Well, the party's over. Now I have to pretend to know a new person's name after I'm introduced to him." I smiled like I imagined a normal person would do in a social situation, and he walked over to take his place at the open chair beside me. I didn't really get a chance to catch his name, because when he sat down to introduce himself, the cheap plastic Adirondack chair he'd chosen collapsed, and all I heard was his scream as his feet flew through the air and a trail of airborne wine illuminated by the firelight followed the arc of his New Balance. Just as his body made contact with the frozen Minnesota earth, I felt a small crack in my exoskeleton, just big enough for an explosive round of uncontrollable laughter to sneak out. I hadn't laughed in so long that I couldn't remember how it worked, but it seemed like the best way to do it was loudly and while pointing at him as he scrambled back to his feet. I couldn't stop once the action began. Moe went inside with whatshisface, and Kevin, who had helped this guy up, giggled along with me for a few moments before regaining his composure. I had no composure. None. Even writing this now, I am giggling alone to myself while I imagine it happening all over again.

Do I always laugh when people fall? Yes. No. Sometimes! Slapstick humor is truly my favorite kind, and as a preternaturally clumsy person, it's usually myself that I'm laughing at. I'd been so self-contained for so long, so careful to keep my grief in check, that I'd kept *everything* in check. There were a few ways to let things out: rage (which the internet was great for), sex (which had already ruined a few lives), and laughter, which was harder to come by than even sex. This moment, spontaneous and strange, sparked something in me. It was an unscripted moment, so out of tune with the usual drudgery of faking it through my grief that I didn't have time to think, I just reacted. I reacted a lot. It was joy that I was experiencing—yes, at this stranger's expense—and it was so sweet I was drunk on it. I was also drunk on wine, and even though Kevin had tried several times to move the conversation forward, and asked me politely to stop laughing, I could not. I laughed until my ribs hurt, until I thought I was going to pass out, throw up, or die. I laughed even when this guy returned from Moe's kitchen, all cleaned up and with a fresh glass of wine. My laughter made him laugh, which made me laugh, which made Moe laugh, which made me laugh more. He righted his chair and tried again. "I'm Matthew," he said, "and I don't know how chairs work."

For weeks, Moe had been insisting that I should meet her friend. Moe and I have different taste in everything. We do not shop in the same sections for clothing or for men. "He's different from my other friends," she kept insisting, "he's a professional." A professional what? She couldn't say. But she knew he had a job! In an office! Downtown! And as enticing as that was, I said no, because, as I explained earlier, I was very busy playing the role of Nora the Internet Dummy Slayer and "a guy with a job" wasn't the best sales pitch I'd ever heard.

In an unexpected turn of events, I spent the rest of the night getting to know the professional friend I had no interest in meeting. He was the guy dressed like a giant toddler, falling out of his chair and spilling wine on himself. He was the guy who didn't seem to mind when I looked at him and burst into laughter, just remembering that he had fallen out of his chair earlier in the night. When the fire was outmatched by the wind chill we moved our party of four inside, and this man and I sat next to each other on a love seat (foreshadowing!!!).

His name was Matthew. His eyes were so giant and blue they looked like cartoon eyeballs. He listened intently to Moe and me while we talked about our dead husbands and our young sons and he laughed at all the right times. At some point, I realized I was being rude and hogging the conversation and I asked him something like, "So, what's up with you?" He seemed startled, like he'd never been asked to talk about himself, and he told me that he was a divorced dad. He had a fourteen-year-old son. A nine-year-old daughter. He'd been separated for five years. I was . . . *fascinated.*

Moe and I have stories that are tragic—her husband died by suicide, mine by cancer—but divorce seemed like a whole different league of emotional suffering, and I had questions. Lots of questions.

Like, "What happened?"

"Then what happened?"

"Then what happened?"

"Oh my GOD; then what happened?"

"Are you SERIOUS?"

He patiently answered all of them, and when my knee brushed his, he moved it immediately like he was a dried-out forest and I was made of pure fire. I figured it must have been a mistake, and tried again. He moved. *Okay*, I thought, *he isn't interested. Yet.*

By 10:30 (which is the latest any social gathering should ever go), we walked out of Moe's house together and to our cars, where we waved good-bye like doofuses until he drove away. I immediately set about trying to find him on Facebook. I knew only his first name—Matthew—which was the fifth most popular boys name in the late seventies, and the fact that he was friends with Moe. I also knew that he was handsome and sweet and honest and not self-conscious and that I would like to have sex with him and possibly even go on a date with him, too, but those were not search criteria I could enter into Facebook.

While my car heated up, I peeled off the bandages on my brand-new tattoos, two small hearts traced from doodles that my late husband Aaron had left on Post-it notes for me during our marriage. Earlier that day, I'd had one permanently etched on each wrist: one facing toward me, and the other away. I'd gotten them on a whim, after snagging a walk-in appointment with the very popular Minneapolis tattoo artist Charlie Forbes, so they symbolize that I am an impulsive person. They also symbolize what I hope to do with the love I learned about from Aaron: give it to others, and to myself. To treat it like a renewable resource and not like Aaron had died and taken the secret recipe with him.

I resisted the urge to scratch my itchy new tattoos and scrolled through all of Moe's friends until I thought I'd found the right Matthew. I couldn't be a hundred percent sure, since he didn't have many public photos, but his profile photo was a portrait drawn in crayon that bore a striking resemblance to the bearded man I'd just met. I wrote a message:

"I think you're cute and funny and you should ask me out sometime."

I waited. I drove home. I brushed my teeth. I waited. I went to sleep. I woke up eight hours later convinced I'd messaged the wrong Matthew. I waited some more, until late that afternoon, my phone vibrated. A reply! I had found the right Matthew. He would love to go out sometime. Numbers were exchanged. A new contact added to my phone.

First name: Matthew

Last name: <3.

Chapter Eight

In Between

We spent a lot of time in the car that first year. Our lives were confined to a pretty small circle in Minneapolis, but I found ways to extend our car trips anyway. We didn't just go to the grocery store, we went to the grocery store on the other side of town, the specialty one that had only twenty percent of what we actually needed. Bonus—it was close enough to a few other grocery stores, which meant more time in the car. I'd happily meet friends for brunch wherever was convenient for *them*. I'd roll onto the freeway just in time for rush hour to start. I was comfortable being on the move, between places, on my way to somewhere, but not quite there yet.

In this period, my entire life was in between. I was heading somewhere but wasn't quite there yet. After Aaron died, I quit my job and decided I would do . . . something else. While this sounds like a very brave choice that I made as an empowered woman, it was more like my job needed me to come back *now*, and I couldn't do that, and so we parted ways in a way that felt mutual but was definitely more like getting dumped by a really polite guy who doesn't want to hurt your feelings. I freelanced and worked on a book. I wasn't a writer quite yet, but I didn't exactly work in advertising anymore, either. I was in between careers.

Ralph and I spent the immediate months after Aaron died living out of a suitcase, flying back and forth across the country to visit friends and family. We'd travel on one-way tickets, so as not to get trapped into a particular itinerary. We'd overstay our welcome in guest rooms and guesthouses. We'd go back to Minneapolis for a few days at a time, only to check our mail and pack some new clothes. We were in between homes.

Our actual house was mostly empty, so I decided to rent it out to friends. I started using my mother's house as our pied-à-terre. We hurriedly packed up the essentials in a few suitcases and boxes, leaving the rest behind for our friends to use. We moved in with my mother on the other side of Minneapolis. Theoretically, this seemed like a great plan: my mom and I would help one another out, and Ralph would have the benefit of a two-grown-up household. In practice, my mom and I were like two strangers who had found each other on Craigslist and agreed to share a home just to cut down on our expenses. I was technically a grown-up and a mom, but I also got into heated arguments with my mother over unloading the dishwasher and putting my shoes away. I was in between teenager and adult.

This wasn't permanent, I knew, but after four months of this return to adolescence, it was too comfortable to be comfortable. My mom and I fell into the best imitation of our typical mother-daughter pattern. If this wasn't permanent—and it couldn't be— then what was the plan? You can't be in between forever.

I am a Realtor's dream: I don't know where I want to live, or what kind of space I want. I'd categorize this as "very open minded" but my Realtor, Dave, indicated that it was a cross between "irritating" and "infuriating." I don't know why. I'd told him very clearly that I was interested in a small bungalow; a Victorian with a big porch; a spare, modern condo; or something mid-century. I was also open to empty lots available for building on, foreclosures and fixer-uppers, maybe an old commercial building that could be rezoned as residential, and that I'd like the place to be in turn-key condition and ready to move into ASAP. My access to HGTV at my mother's house had made me the most insufferable kind of guest on *House Hunters,* the kind of person who insists that they need space for entertaining and seven bedrooms, who has to have the granite countertop and the apron sink, who wants character but only the kind of character that looks good on Pinterest. My Realtor is also my brother's father-in-law, so the more I strained him, the more I strained several other relationships within my family. Because my dad was dead, Dave also had to be my stand-in father figure. He had everything a dad should have: a mustache, a deep bench of Dad Jokes for every occasion, and strong opinions about every home that came across during our MLS searches.

"Why don't you consider renting?" Dave said after I rejected about fifteen potential houses based on the fact that none of them had a fireplace, which had not previously been on my must-have list of criteria. I refused. Rent? I was already renting! I mean, I didn't pay my mother any money, but she was essentially my landlord. Renting was just another form of in between, a semicolon where I needed a period. I needed Ralph to feel like we had a spot in this world that was really ours, a place to call our own. A place to come home to. I knew that what I was doing, by constantly moving, was avoiding putting roots down in the fear that they wouldn't take hold. Or that they would, and I'd get chopped down again.

We started our search in downtown Minneapolis, the land of

shiny condos and warehouses converted into loft spaces. A condo would be perfect for us, I had decided. No lawn for me to mow, and no snow for me to shovel. Underground parking during the bitter Minnesota winters, and plenty of security. Ralph could ride his bike on the polished concrete floors, and we'd spend our Saturday mornings walking to the local cafe for doughnuts and hot chocolate. We didn't need much space. It was just the two of us after all.

When I was in fifth grade, I begged my parents to buy me a hermit crab. It was a gross request, but they honored it, and soon I was the happy owner of a sad crustacean that had no business living in Minnesota. The pet store had recommended we buy some extra shells for it, so it could move into something bigger as it grew. We didn't get any extra shells, because they cost money, and eventually my hermit crab died of mysterious causes. I couldn't tell you what did him (her?) in, but I can tell you that when I looked at these sleek, small condos, something inside of me said "no."

It wasn't just the association fees—although, what the actual hell, those are like a second mortgage payment—it was the clear vision of what my life with Ralph would look like living in a place like that. A two-bedroom condo was enough room for just Ralph and me. We were a good team with a good life together, but we weren't built to be a duo. Aaron and I had planned on more children. The exact number was never officially agreed upon, but my goal was four. Four was a nice even number that would give Ralph the same number of siblings that I had. Four is chaos in childhood and comfort as an adult. I needed to give us what I hadn't given to my hermit crab, may it Rest in Peace: a space big enough to grow into. A space to thrive. A space that was bigger than a condo.

So we moved on down the checklist to the million other combinations I was open to, driving to what seemed like a million open houses. Dave was infinitely patient.

"Before we get too far down the path," Dave said in his Professional Voice, "let's get you pre-approved for a mortgage."

Pre-approval sounds fun. Maybe because it has my favorite word in it? I love approval. I seek it from basically any and everyone. Being pre-approved sounded like there was even more approval on the horizon, and this was just a formality: a way for the bank to look me up and down and say, "Yep, we like what we see, come on back in a few weeks for some more affirmations and validations." Unfortunately, the bank did not like what they saw. They didn't see the brave, recently widowed woman who was pursuing her dream of being a writer and who was totally, one hundred percent going to succeed. What they saw was an unemployed widow trying to buy a house without a solid, steady income. Both were accurate ways of looking at me, but I preferred the first view.

Ever since that pesky economic crash of 2008, banks have gotten reeeeeeeally upright about handing out mortgages to people who say, "Trust me, I'll pay it." They need, like, real proof. On paper, I was not a great candidate for a house, so I had to get beyond a computerized application. I needed to meet face-to-face with someone, to look them in the eye and say out loud, "Trust me, I'll pay it."

It didn't work.

I did not have a mortgage pre-approval, or even pre-pre-approval. So, of course, that's when I found the perfect house: a white two-story with black shutters and bright boughs of flowers spilling over from the window boxes. There was a pergola in the backyard, and an actual picket fence. The house itself was surrounded by a towering hedge of lilacs, which gave the backyard a Secret Garden vibe. It looked exactly like a dollhouse a friend had bought for Ralph at a garage sale, so that's how I instantly started referring to it. The Dollhouse. It was just a few blocks away from my little brother and his family. The for-sale sign was so fresh that the house wasn't even listed online yet. I called Dave. "I found the perfect house. Find out how much it costs and offer them a little more than that."

Dave insisted that I look *inside* the house before I made an offer, but I already knew. I already saw our Christmas tree in the front window, and tiny American flags lining the walkway on the fourth of July. I already saw Ralph and me building a snowman in the front yard and shoveling the walkway together. Not just the two of us, but more of us . . . a bigger version of our team, filling out the space. This house was as boring and traditional as houses could be, the kind of house a child would draw if you said "Draw me a house." This was a house that a family would live in. And instead of seeing Ralph and myself as two pieces of rubble, I saw us for what we were: a family. Even without Aaron, we were still a family. A small family, yes, but a family. Those little condos didn't feel right because they weren't right, because our family was meant to grow. I didn't know how, or when, but I knew that it would happen in this house. That this house, even with its aging furnace and the spider-filled basement, would be where we let ourselves grow.

"This doesn't have a big bathtub, a porch, a new roof, an attached garage, a finished basement, a gas fireplace, or any of the things that you said were must-haves yesterday," Dave said. "And this kitchen is a disaster." I gave him the kind of hug I used to give my dad, pinning his arms to his sides and squeezing until I felt him give up.

"It's perfect. I have to have it," I replied and started a mental calculation of how many gallons of paint it would take to cover the baby-poop brown that covered the kitchen walls.

"You have to have a mortgage approval," he countered. "It's bad form to make an offer you can't pay."

I did my best to look employed and responsible at the meeting. I wore a skirt and a shirt that had buttons. I put on makeup and pulled my hair back. I sat down across from Richard the Mortgage Guy and started my pitch: "I'm widowed, I'm determined, I'm buying this goddamn house." That's the headline, at least. The actual "pitch" was more like me rambling, waving my hands around, and possibly even begging.

Ten minutes in, just when I was getting to the part where I knew I had found the right house for my son and me to start over in, Richard raised his hand to interject. "Do you have your tax returns?" he asked me, and I reached into my bag to wrestle out the stack of backup information I had compiled: five years of tax returns, bank statements, and check stubs from my shiny new freelance career.

"This is possible . . ." he said, punching some numbers into his computer. "It won't be traditional, but it's *possible*."

Richard needed a few days to pitch my case to the rest of the credit union. He apologized, but the process took time. Would I mind, he wondered, waiting in that kind of limbo?

Of course, I didn't mind. I'd heard him loud and clear: it was *possible*. Yes, this was more in between, but it was a new kind of in between for me. This in between was joyful. This uncertainty was one that had a beautiful new beginning on the other side.

Chapter Nine

Ready or Not

The psychic was hired to tell the fortunes of five ten-year-old Catholic school girls. You'd think she would try to tailor her message to the audience, maybe gloss over some things, cut some corners, keep things on the positive side—tell all of us that we could expect long and happy lives with handsome husbands and healthy children.

You'd be wrong.

"Interesting," she said while she looked into my eyes. "You will have two husbands. Both great loves. With one, you'll be very poor. With the other, you'll be rich." At the time, I looked a lot like Jonathan Taylor Thomas and Macaulay Culkin had a baby together. I wore primarily turtlenecks and coordinating sweat suits. I was often mistaken for a boy, and I had no idea why, because bowl cuts were equally popular among and hideous on boys and girls in equal measure. I was mostly concerned with my fortune for the next week or so, not the next twenty years. I needed to know whether Gene liked me back, and if my basketball team would ever win a game. And here this lady was talking to me about husbands? Sure, I figured I'd be married someday, but I assumed a husband would just be assigned to me, perhaps in college or even high school. *A* husband. Two husbands just didn't make any sense, mathematically or otherwise. You could only ever be married to one person; everyone knew that!

The word *divorce* would not enter my vocabulary until the next year, when my friend Samantha sat cross-legged on her daybed, tears streaming down her face. Her parents' living room—her mom's living room, now—was filled with boxes of her dad's belongings. Her dad would still be her dad, but he was moving out. I walked across the street to my own house feeling frozen and afraid, and watched my parents warily, looking for any cracks in their relationship that may result in my dad getting a sad apartment and growing a ponytail. Divorce meant that Samantha's house became a place where we could hang out unsupervised on Friday nights while her mother went on dates with men who seemed too old and too sad to be anyone's "boyfriend." But I didn't know any of this the night of the party. I only knew that my friend Kate's familiar living room had been transformed by the presence of this all-seeing woman with her intense eye contact and incense. I had chills all over my body as she closed my fingers around my palm and gently motioned for the next girl to enter the room.

An hour before, I'd been a regular fourth grader, hoping I could get my ears pierced. Now, I was a girl who had seen my own weird future. I don't remember what the other girls' fortunes were, but I do remember that when we were all snuggled up in the basement in our dorky nightgowns, eating popcorn and watching Olson Twins movies we were definitely too old for, repeating my fortune for them turned them all into the human equivalent of a grimace emoji.

My parents were not big fans of sleepovers. "You have your own bed to sleep in," my dad would rant, "and that's where you belong."

They didn't appreciate the sleepover hangover caused by Pizza Hut and daring one another to stay up past midnight. Their enthusiasm was not increased by my bounding into the house the next morning to tell them about my brush with the supernatural. My dad's normally stern face froze solid while I told him about my psychic reading. "A psychic," he said with disdain, "told you what?!" I repeated it for him, more slowly this time, so he could comprehend it. A psychic told me I would have two husbands.

"Well!" he proclaimed. "That's some bullshit."

I was immediately embarrassed for myself, my friend, and my future husbands. My dad was only a strict Catholic when it was one of the major holidays or when he was annoyed with something, and this was just the kind of thing to rile up his religion. "What kind of a person tells a little girl she'll get married twice?!" His quarrel seemed not only to be with the idea of being married twice, which implied eventual divorce, but with the entire method by which she came to this vision of my future. He declared it all—the psychic, the birthday party, the sleepover, and the reading—total bullshit.

This had been a fun birthday party, but it wasn't a life-changing event for me. By that age, I was already enamored with the idea of the supernatural. I was a child who lunged for the Variety section of the *Minneapolis Star-Tribune* every morning, flipping to the funny pages, where the horoscopes lived. I was, and am, *such* a Capricorn: ambitious, stubborn, loyal. I read my horoscopes half for fun, and half because who *doesn't* want a little help understanding their place in this world? I was being raised to believe in a Holy Trinity: God, Jesus, The Holy Spirit. I was being raised to believe in a series of saints, and to pray a rosary. I was not being raised to believe in astrology, but is it really such a leap between the two?

I grew up to be the kind of adult woman who sees an energy healer and cleanses my children's auras, which is like saying I grew up to be a soccer mom: the two are interchangeable, and a hugely overlapping Venn diagram. I grew up to be the kind of woman who prays to God, and who lights Palo Santo in the mornings to set my intentions. I grew up to be the kind of woman who believes in spiritual pluralism, a sort of cafeteria approach to faith and religion that puts about as much stock in my star chart and my own self as I do in a benevolent (and probably female) God. It's all just different ways to make sense of the world around us, and our place in it. We are who we are maybe because of some big, omniscient force, because of when and where the planets were in relation to when and where we were born, because of our own choices and actions . . . because of a lot of things that nobody can really know for sure.

Let me say right now that it's a good thing my dad is already dead, or this chapter would for sure kill him. The man's *dying wish* was for "generations of Catholic McInernys" and I just started going to a—gasp!!—Lutheran church.

I mostly forgot about this prophecy, until I was in my mid-twenties, and for some reason decided to bring it up to my then boyfriend. We had reached a point where we should have been talking about marriage and kids but weren't. I pretended that it was because I was just a very modern woman who didn't care about conventional family life, but really I was just pretending that this was a viable relationship with a person who did not share my goals or values. I thought he'd find this little piece of my childhood funny, but he was actually deeply offended by this view of my future. He didn't like the way it sounded: that I'd fall in deep love twice, but that one relationship would be poor, and the other wealthier. In his mind, I'd been programmed at age ten to be a gold-digger, and disclosing this prediction to him was my way of telling him that he was not going to be my one true love. I was stunned because:

1. He was actually irritated by a birthday-party psychic from the Midwest and

2. I made more money than any man I ever dated, including him, making me the world's least effective gold-digger.

Either way, this disclosure haunted the guy. It became the thing he brought up over and over and over again, mostly when he was drunk or high, which was basically always. Why would he marry me if I was just going to move on to someone rich?

If you can believe it, that boyfriend was not one of my big loves and we did not get married. And I am not divorced, or rich.*

But I *did* get married twice. I *do* have two big loves.

Here is what I don't believe in: I don't believe that God has an itinerary-like plan for everyone, that she's sitting up there in a cloud, pointing at us like, "You get cancer! You get a fancy house! You get a fancy house *and* cancer!" I don't believe that the psychic at Kate's tenth birthday party was truly telling my future. Or maybe I do.

Because I remembered that party, sharply, in more detail, after Aaron died. Long before I was ready to think about ever loving another human being again, I remembered being told that I would marry twice, I remembered my father's reaction.

I know a lot of people who know a lot of dead people; it's something I tend to bond over when I meet someone. Once, I was talking with a friend whose husband had also died young. He was a lot like Aaron—preternaturally positive and happy and *present*—and

---

* Yet. I need this psychic to come through on that part of the prediction, and I would prefer not to hear the interpretation that she was telling me that I would be rich in immaterial goods. For all this stress, she could at least foresee some good old-fashioned monetary wealth, right??

she wondered: Did a part of him know he was going to die young? Somewhere deep inside, was his soul aware that he was here for a good time, not a long time? I had wondered the same thing about Aaron. And the same thing about myself. Because that little girl who was reading her horoscope was a little girl who lived with a sense of dread about the future, who laid in bed crying about the eventual end of the world, when everything was just particles, and worried that maybe her particles would drift away from her family's particles and be lonely out there in an ever-expanding universe. There was certainly something in me, from a young age, that knew that life was going to be hard. Yes, I desperately needed therapy, but it was the early nineties and that wasn't really a thing yet. At least not in Minnesota.

Maybe everything that psychic said *was* bullshit. Maybe it's all bullshit. But some of it is bullshit I can believe in.

Like many older white men, my father was certain that he had all the answers to life. These were answers that he would swiftly, decisively, and loudly gift to me and my siblings, at his own discretion, looking up from his crossword puzzle to share a withering glance and pelt us with a small kernel of wisdom. Often, these pieces of wisdom began with some variation of "the problem with people your age . . ." before offering the actionable advice you were seeking. If you're wondering what the problem with people your age is (whatever your age), I can only tell you from my father's observations that it could be anything at all. I usually zoned out a little during his monologues, but I recall him blaming the shortcomings of any generation but his own on overbearing parents (he, himself, could never be accused of such nonsense), participation ribbons, unrealistic depictions of the female body in media targeted to children, poor diet, and general laziness.

Of all the times my dad's voice turned into the horn sound like the grown-ups in a *Peanuts* cartoon, most of them I've forgotten. But I can still hear his most useful piece of advice. "The problem with people," he said, a vast generalization not targeted to my age group, which may have been why I kept listening, "is that they think there's a right time for things. They think the world gives a shit about your timing." Maybe this was why the psychic had bristled him so much: because the idea that the future was predictable was just as ridiculous as the idea that there was a specific chronology you could follow on your way to happiness, that there was a right time for marriage, or children, or buying a minivan. That was pure nonsense to him.

I was three weeks late entering this world, and I think being so overdue ensured that an acute awareness of time was ingrained in my DNA. Time seemed always to be moving too fast, and I felt perpetually behind. There was a lot to do, and not a lot of time to do it. Aside from my father, the entire world seemed to reinforce this: we had standardized tests twice a year to prove we were learning; we got report cards every quarter. There were always tests to take, and teams to make. And that was in grade school! Middle school would prove more intense: We'd have lockers! We'd need to get good grades so we could get into good high schools and good colleges and have a good life. Life was like an endless to-do list with a very specific order. My dad was wrong. The path to happiness was clear and finite: get good grades, go to college, get a good job, fall in love, get married, have children, work until you die. What was wrong with that?

If my older brother was an animal, he would be a sloth. Thoughtful, deliberate, and very loyal. I don't know if sloths are actually loyal, but don't they seem like they would be? Austin dated his wife, Lori, for ten years before he proposed, and this drove my father absolutely bonkers. What was Austin waiting for, a sign from God? Well, Austin was waiting to be done with grad school, to be financially secure, and also . . . I don't know, you can't hurry love or a sloth. My parents were married at twenty-four, mostly because, look, I don't want to rush to any conclusions, *but* their wedding was in July and my sister was born the following January, a giant, very full-term baby. That being said, my father always romanticized their love story. How they were married before they'd finished college. How they moved into a run-down house just off the freeway, where my mother was once robbed at knifepoint by a man whose face was covered by pantyhose, which I bet you thought happened only in movies. This guy threw my mom into the basement and locked the door while my sister slept in her crib, blissfully unaware. How money came and went, and more kids came, and more money went, and they figured everything out together, as it happened. He hadn't even had a checking account before he and my mother got married, but they were happy, and they had each other.

Life had worked out for my parents, and their solid marriage and their four not-terrible children were enough evidence for my dad that the secret to happiness is to let it just happen. Or, at the very least, not to expect life to comply with your expectations. Even if you never want to be married or have babies, even if you want to keep all your money in a shoebox under your bed for eternity, there's something to be said for letting go of the idea that you can engineer life to your specifications.

That's what my dad was trying to teach us. He wasn't telling us that we had to want the same things that he and my mom had (marriage, children, a vacation home to snowbird to), but that we couldn't let timing be an excuse for not getting the things that we did want. Waiting for the perfect conditions is a waste of what limited time you have on this earth. What Aaron and I had together may not have been our first choice—was not really even a choice at all—but it was good. We made it into the best version of the worst situation, and we made it happen regardless of what the future held. I married Aaron not knowing if he would live for three months or three years. We had a baby together not knowing that Aaron's tumor would return right before I gave birth. Aaron died at age thirty-five, and while there is no disputing that it was the wrong time for him to die, we could look each other in the eye and say, "We did good."

But now Aaron was gone. My dad was gone. And the only person whose eyes I could look into anymore were Ralph's. Ralph was only two when all this happened, so he thought I was good at everything. It's a true blessing that a toddler doesn't know when you're swimming in a sea of self-doubt. They don't know when you're at the end of your rapidly fraying rope or when you are duct-taping your world together and hoping it holds for another day. Ralph didn't know that I was unemployed. He didn't know that I was making it up as I went, and neither did most people. I really had felt ready for anything with Aaron, because his bravery made me look so much braver than I actually was. I didn't have to do the brain surgeries, or the chemo. It wasn't my body being radiated. It wasn't my life ending. We had each other, and the threat of Aaron's death to inspire us to keep pushing forward. I didn't feel that way at all anymore after he was gone, but I learned to do a good job faking it. The conditions weren't perfect, but they were still better than most. I had a dead husband and a lot of debt and a child, but I am also white and middle class and educated and American. As far as I fell, there was still always going to be something below me to break the fall.

Here is what my dad was right about: there is not a right time for everything, or anything really. I know that because I have lived the reality, and have seen others live the same way. Here is what my dad didn't say: that it's easy to accept that notion when you're a good, safe distance from the difficult experience you're living through. It's easy to say "everything happens for a reason" when you've already found your reason. It's easy to say that timing is irrelevant when you're looking back at the hardest things in your life. It's a lot damn harder when you're in the thick of it, when you can't even see where your next step is. I wanted the comfort and safety of perspective. I wanted to open my eyes and be five years into the future, to know that whatever happened next was going to be different from my current reality, that even if Matthew's arrival was terribly timed, it didn't matter anyway.

It didn't matter if I saw *Game of Thrones* spoilers on Twitter. I still wept for every Stark. It didn't matter that I knew how Aaron's stage-four brain cancer would eventually end. It doesn't matter for you that I married Matthew, and had his baby, and the six of us live in a house in the suburbs of Minneapolis. (There's your spoiler.) A spoiler may ruin the surprise, but it can't save you from the shock, and it can't prepare you for what's next. What's next is unknowable, but one thing is certain: it doesn't care about what you want, or what you're expecting. It doesn't care whether a psychic tipped you off at a birthday party in fourth grade or if it catches you completely off guard. It's coming for you, ready or not.

Chapter Ten

Smile

I guess I looked too sad for a widow. I definitely didn't look happy enough for the drunk man who was swaying in front of me. His opening line was a bold one.

"I've been watching you all night," he slurred, and I felt my face contort into the shape that every woman instinctively knows to make in this situation: a stiff smile that says "Okay, I acknowledge your presence but can this exchange be over now?" I turned away from him, and signaled to my friend to cover for me, but he leaned over her, because he wasn't done talking.

"Look," he tried to whisper, "I know you're a nice person, but you don't look very nice tonight." At that second, I sent daggers flying out of my eyeballs toward him while he closed his eyes as if in prayer to the Gods of Drunken Wisdom. Then, he said it. "You should . . . smile." He smiled for me, nice and big, demonstrating how exactly to turn the corners of my mouth up. I contemplated the consequences of punching him at a nonprofit fund-raiser.

Oh, yes. Some context. This wasn't a bar scene. This entire exchange took place at the folding table where I had been standing for hours representing Still Kickin, the nonprofit I started in honor of my dead husband. Now, this wasn't a fancy affair. We don't do big, sit-down dinners with cold chicken and silent auctions. We just provide financial support to people going through the worst in life, and raise the money through sales of our apparel, all of which proudly proclaims to the world that you're still here, Still Kickin. It's work that means a lot to me, even if it doesn't pay me anything, because it means I get to be there for other people the way they were there for me and Aaron and Ralph. It also means a lot of public crying, which is what I had been doing that entire night. I listened to people tell me about their dead moms and their dead dads. About a sister struggling with drug abuse, and a sick nephew who was going to spend his entire short life in the hospital. I hadn't spent the whole night frowning, I had spent it crying with people who needed to cry and raising money to help people who needed help.

Did the world need another nonprofit? No. Did it need a nonprofit run by two women, my friend Lindsay and me, with absolutely no experience in the nonprofit world? I assure you, it did not.

But you can blame Aaron for that. This was all his idea.

It was inspired by his favorite T-shirt. His cancer. His big, generous heart and creative spirit. His wish to give other people what the world had given us: the ability to be seen without pity. And money. Money is super helpful when your life is falling apart. Aaron had the idea but ran out of time. All I had to do was usher this idea across the finish line, to make my husband's dying wish into a reality.

Aaron's favorite T-shirt was a threadbare cotton shirt in a faded kelly green. There is no tag, no size. Just two faded and cracked words printed across the front: STILL KICKIN. He bought it at a secondhand store in the heyday of the ironic T-shirt era. While other people were sporting faux-aged JESUS IS MY HOMEBOY shirts, Aaron was amassing a collection of weathered little league, family re-union, and novelty tees from Minnesota's thrift stores. The green Still Kickin one was a favorite and part of a small collection I wasn't allowed to borrow. As a very hygienic and good-smelling person, Aaron's main concern was that I was overly sweaty and would per-manently pit-stain it, which was fair. As a naturally thin person, his secondary concern was that I may stretch it out. In the arms. This was also a fair concern, though I would like to tell any straight man reading this that there are better ways to tell a girlfriend that your shirt is off-limits.

This favorite T-shirt was the one he was wearing on the day he had that first seizure and was rushed from the floor of his cubicle to the local hospital. That silly, faded T-shirt, with its crackled let-ters, wasn't as funny as it had been when Aaron wore it in ironically good health. Now it was meaningful and important. We hung it in Aaron's closet like it was a tuxedo and busted it out for chemo and radiation appointments. It made the nurses laugh, and it made us feel safe and strong.

Our fellow patients would shuffle or be wheeled in, and you would know instantly that you were looking at a shadow of what they had once been. Aaron's full-time job came with insurance that covered the medications that some of our brain cancer comrades had to petition and beg for. They'd eye Aaron's T-shirt and give him their version of a smile and a thumbs-up, and we'd step into the unknown of Aaron's appointment feeling fortunate, no matter what was coming our way in the next twenty minutes.

Aaron's idea was this: replicate that thrift-store T-shirt, sell it online, and give the money to . . . somewhere! Brain cancer research made a lot of sense, because it's underfunded. It also felt worth ac-knowledging that there are countless ways for life to kick you in the gonads, and for anything related to Aaron to be unconventional and big-hearted and unique. Aaron died just after the shirt launched, and those two words then took on a life of their own. People set up an online fundraiser and helped me pay off our medical debt and cover Aaron's funeral expenses. His funeral was a sea of green Still Kickin shirts, and people kept buying them. Not because they knew Aaron personally, but because those words meant something to them. They bought them to celebrate the struggles and successes we all eventually experience. I knew that Aaron had been right: this deserved to be its own thing. And I knew I had been right, too: it didn't need to be about brain cancer. Or cancer. It didn't need to be about any specific thing, other than plain old surviving this crazy world.

All of my work revolves around the hard things in life. I have made it my actual job to just think and write and talk about the crappy things in life that other people don't want to talk about, and to listen to them, too. That last part is important because it's a hard thing to do. It's hard to sit with someone's pain and allow it to make you uncomfortable. It's much easier to try to fill that hole in the conversation with small talk, or hand the person a tissue instead of offering them your shoulder. It's much easier to implore them to see the bright side than to be in the darkness with them. I get it. I've done it. I still do it. Being a tragedy connoisseur does not make me a tragedy expert, and I still fuck it up sometimes.

Just a few months after Aaron died, my cousin Tommy killed himself. He was the same age as my big brother, and I'd spent my childhood looking up to him. Tommy was clever and funny and cool, and sometimes he let me play with his action figures. As a grown-up, I knew that his life had turned out harder than mine, but I didn't understand it, and I didn't ask questions. At his funeral, I hugged his mother and father and then . . . I heard myself talking.

Why was I talking? Why was I trying to explain the unexplainable? Why was I trying to pretend anyone could ever understand this, that what the family had been waiting for was an inexpert opinion from an emotionally distant cousin who had no experience in suicide or severe mental illness? Why had I instantly turned into everyone I had wanted to punch at Aaron's funeral? Everyone who told me that it would be okay, or that he was at peace now?

Because I was uncomfortable. If we struggle with what to say when someone dies of cancer, we're absolutely dumbstruck when they die of mental illness. I wanted to make my aunt and uncle feel better, so that I could feel better. I didn't want to be sad, even if that was what the moment called for. Accessing that feeling would mean accessing my grief for Aaron, and my dad, and the baby who should have been a month old by now.

But back to that room. That fundraiser. That guy. I don't know the motivations of the drunk man insisting that I smile while soaking up the traumas of strangers. I don't know if he's an operative for Big Patriarchy or just a run-of-the-mill buffoon. He's probably a mix of both. And I think he's also just a person who thought that he could smooth over the awkwardness of acknowledging my pain by pushing me to fake my own happiness for the sake of his own comfort.

On any other day, in any other year, maybe I would have just smiled for him and then called him an asshole behind his back. But I was tired of smiling, and tired of pretending to be happy and okay. I'd spent almost a year pretending. I was exhausted. And even though my smile made everyone else more comfortable being around a young widow, that night, crying with a bunch of people in public? That was the most comfortable I'd been all year. I told him our conversation was over, and Lindsay tagged me out of the booth.

Here's the thing: even if I hadn't spent the night knee-deep in the feelings of others, even if my husband was alive and well and at home with our two living children . . . I didn't owe that guy a smile.

What he may have thought was a light flirtation, or good-natured small talk, is actually an exhausting part of being a woman. I can count the number of times I've told a man to smile on zero hands, because I've never done it. I cannot count the number of times I've been told to smile, because math doesn't go that high. And for every man (and there's always one) who is like, "hey, this happens to men, too!" . . .

1. hush. The women are talking now and

2. I'm going to go out on a limb here and guess that you're the kind of guy who is perplexed when you tell someone to "smile," "relax," or "calm down" and find those words have the exact opposite effect.

Here's a newsflash, my male friends. "Smile" is not a way to actually cheer a person up. It's a way to tell them "please adjust your face to my preferences." And it isn't expected of men the way it is of women. No matter how mainstream feminism may be now, the message that girls owe the world is that the appearance of happiness is everywhere. Browse through the message tees in any retailer and notice how the word *happy* is a staple in any girls' department, and completely absent from the boys' department. Notice that men who don't constantly smile have faces, and women who don't constantly smile are afflicted with "Resting Bitch Face," a curious physical ailment that seems to have spread of late like a case of foot and mouth does through a preschool class. Remember how Hillary Clinton was diagnosed with RBF for not smiling enough during the presidential debates, and alternately described as crazy, grandmotherly, or condescending when she smiled too much. It's so much fun to be a woman!

"Ugh," a stranger commented on my Facebook post about this night, "now we can't just want a woman to be happy?"

Of course you can want us to be happy, fella! And you can help make us happy, too! You could start by insisting on pay equity, particularly for women of color. You could continue by hushing your sweet little mouth on topics like reproductive rights. You could believe survivors of sexual assault. And if it's not too much trouble, smile? As for me, I'm Still Kickin. Keep it up, and I may just aim for your chin.

Chapter Eleven

Sophie's Hot Dad

People always want to know if Aaron and I talked about dating after he died, if he gave me his blessing to fall in love again, to build a new family. The answer is . . . sort of? Weirdly enough, while my husband was dying, I wasn't really thinking about my romantic future. My romantic present—a husband being ravaged by brain cancer, and a toddler who would grow up without him—gave us both plenty to think about and talk about. One of the best gifts that Aaron and I gave each other was having hard conversations: we set healthcare directives and wills, we established power of attorney and talked about what our wishes were for end-of-life care. When Aaron died, I didn't have to wonder about what he wanted: we'd written his obituary together, we'd talked about his funeral, and he'd told me where he kept his funeral playlist.

I list those things off as if they're a grocery list, but at the time they were gut-wrenching conversations. Because for me and most people, talking about our funeral is an abstract. But for Aaron, it was real. It was coming soon. Our best conversations about life and death happened the same way all our best conversations about *any-thing* happened: with a joke. His obituary started with the two of us in bed in choked-up silence, my fingers hovering over the keyboard. I went first.

"Purmort, Aaron Joseph, age whatever, was murdered by his angry wife after forgetting garbage day for the third week in a row."

Aaron laughed his signature laugh, the one where his shoulders shimmied, and his nose wrinkled.

"Purmort, Aaron Joseph, age whatever . . . died of complications from a radioactive spider bite."

"YES!"

There it was. We riffed from there, my fingers flying over the keyboard while he rattled on, and when it was over, I read it aloud, and we both laughed and wiped tears from our faces.

"There's no way in hell they'll print that," he said, and I shrugged.

My dad had died just a few weeks before, and he made sure that everything he said in those final weeks could be some unbeatable dying words. Sitting beside him in the ICU a few days before he died, my dad beckoned me closer.

"When I die," he whispered, "make sure you help your mom with her Match.com profile. I caught a glimpse of it and it's not looking good."

My mom gasped, the joke entirely lost on her. The nurses froze in awkward silence. And my dad and Aaron busted out in laughter.

A kindness that Aaron and I gave to one another was pretending that it was anyone's guess which of us would die first. It made our hard conversations easier. I wasn't just asking *him* to make a will, I was making one myself. I wasn't just asking about his medical directives, I was writing my own, too.

I turned to Aaron and told him that if I were to die first, the only thing I would want was for him to be happy. Alone, and pining for me the rest of his life.

He laughed and agreed to my terms.

"Just don't date anyone funnier than me," he said. "Or who wears sweatpants. Or cargo pants. Don't date any boring dads."

MY SISTER HAD INSISTED ON knowing the first and last name of the man I was going to dinner with, so she could do some preliminary Googling, and offer her opinions. Whatever she found after I texted her Matthew's full name was important enough that she called me.

"Nora!" she shouted, "you're going on a date with Sophie's Hot Dad!"

It turns out the social circles Matthew and I frequented had another overlap: his daughter, Sophie, was in Girl Scouts with my niece Trixie. Sophie and Trixie had attended each other's birthday parties. They were friends! And Matthew was Sophie's Hot Dad, so named because of his obvious handsomeness and because it's universally appealing to see a man take on the parental duties associated with Girl Scouts. My sister had only had a handful of conversations with Matthew over the past few years, but she insisted that he wasn't just any dad, he was a *really good* dad. And yeah, he was hot. He had a brooding look to him, like he probably spent a lot of time in high school reading philosophy and listening to The Smiths, and not a lot of time going on dates, which I learned on our first date was an uncannily accurate description of his high school experience.

There is nothing strange about comparing a new potential suitor to your former loves. I have done this on every single first date I've ever been on. It might not be fair, to expect someone new to meet or exceed a standard that another person had months or even years to set, but it's practically inevitable. I did it when I met Aaron, flabbergasted at how easily he stepped over my very, very low bars for male interaction.

I didn't want to compare Matthew to Aaron, but the timelines of each romance aligned in a way that made it impossible not to. A year before, I'd been sitting in bed with Aaron writing his obituary, and now twelve months later, I was sitting in a restaurant waiting for a man who was at least ten minutes late for dinner.

Aaron would never be late. Minus ten points.

Matthew arrived, twelve minutes late* and completely soaked. Last year, I'd given Aaron a piggyback over a snowbank to our favorite diner for what we didn't know would be his last meal out. This year, it was pouring rain.

Stop. I told myself. *Be here.*

The first year of widowhood is a year of firsts: 365 days where you can say "last year, we were . . ." The blank is filled in with everything from the monumental to the mundane: we were at the oncologist for an MRI, we were picking apples at the orchard and pretending he wasn't dying, we were looking at the price of flights to Arizona for a Christmas he would never celebrate. It's an entire calendar year of emotional landmines, every single day loaded with meaning. I'd wanted to propose a different day for our first date, but which one? If every day was reserved for living in my past, when would I have time for the present?

Two hours after Matthew *finally* arrived, our dinner was over and the staff at Pizza Nea was ready to go home. Around the time

---

* During the proofreading process, Matthew requested that I point out that one of his greatest regrets is being late for our first date. He would also like to point out that he has not been late for anything since then.

our appetizers arrived, I'd stopped cataloging the differences between Matthew and Aaron, and slipped into the present moment. It was not an intentional shift; it was an imperceptible magnetic pull into the present moment, probably emanating from Matthew's unbelievably blue eyes. They were crinkled at the edges, and lined with jet black lashes that only men are born with because the world is unfair. His eyes said, *I'm listening.* And also, *Make out with the man attached to these eyeballs.*

My first date with Aaron had lasted for hours. We'd gone from a dinner to a concert to sitting outside on the curb after the coffee shop closed, to texting one another until I fell asleep next to my phone. My time with Matthew felt like catching up with an old friend, and I didn't want the night to be over.

To be around Aaron was to feel like you were a part of something special, even if the something special was just a two a.m. trip to a shitty diner.

I knew after a few hours with Matthew that he had never once been the life of the party. He had been at parties, probably, but was the quiet guy in the corner you assumed was probably a snobby jerk because he wasn't talking to anyone, when in reality he was just trying to will his body to teleport him back to his apartment. He was built for one-on-one conversations, or a small group setting. It was adorable. *He* was adorable. Those Girl Scouts moms didn't call him Sophie's Hot Dad for nothing.

When dinner was over, we had stepped outside into an unseasonable downpour. What should have been snow was a deluge of rain that neither of us were dressed for. I pretended to look for a taxi when Matthew gestured toward his car, parked just up the street. Maybe the date wasn't over?

And then we got to his car. I don't know or care about cars, so I'm not judging the kind of car he drives. I'm also a person whose car is littered with stale McDonald's fries, so I'm not judging his cleanliness, either. I'm judging how quickly he destroyed my fantasies about him.

"Oh my God," I screamed the moment I closed the car door, "you *smoke*?!"

Wrapped up in my disappointment was also a little relief. It didn't matter that I'd just spent two hours absorbed in conversation with a pair of eyeballs. It didn't matter that we had sped through two hours of dinner with ease, the conversation pausing only long enough for us to shove some food in our mouths while we jumped from topic to topic like we were old friends who hadn't seen each other for eons, and not strangers just starting to get to know one another. Here was my out: a cancer wife like me could not possibly fall in love with a man who thumbed his nose at good sense, who was so flagrantly careless with his own health, who engaged in something so filthy. That's what I told him, too. I would *never* date a smoker.

Matthew gave me a guilty look.

"I hardly ever smoke," he lied.

"I don't care," I shrugged. "I won't date a smoker."

He sighed heavily, and I expected I'd be getting a Lyft home. Instead, he started the car and flicked on his signal, eyeing his mirror for an opening in traffic.

"Well," he said, easing onto Hennepin Avenue, "then I guess I don't smoke anymore."

WHY TO DATE A DAD

Or a mom. A parent in general, really, but the
title was better with alliteration.

I've been a mom since 2013. Matthew has been a dad since 2001 (yes, I am a younger woman. No, not by much. He was basically a teen dad). I don't think I ever would have found Matthew online, for a few reasons:

1. He is five-ten but insists he is five-eleven. This is a very common practice for men, and since I've been six feet tall since eighth grade, I know that most men overestimate their height by at least an inch. As such, I've always set my parameters to a six-two minimum, knowing I'll get a guy around my height. This is not important to me because I need to feel small and dainty next to my man, but because the closer a guy is to my size, the more likely it is for his clothes to fit me. This is purely an economical preference.

2. I would have never seen "father of a teen and a tween" and swiped whatever direction means yes.

The loss would have been entirely mine, obviously, because Matthew's dadness is what makes him such a good partner for me. If it were ethical, I would just loan him out to every single and searching woman I could so she could see what she's missing by taking dads out of the equation. Instead, I'll just implore you all to open your eyes, search criteria, and hearts to include parents . . . for these enticing reasons.

THEY'RE NOT GOING TO WASTE YOUR TIME. They don't *have* any time to waste. Because soccer pickup is at 7:30 p.m. and there's an orchestra concert on Saturday and school pictures are coming up and the lunches need to be packed. If it's not going to work, you're gonna know *real quick*.

THEY'LL (GENTLY) CHECK YOUR EGO. If you have come of age in the era of Taylor Swift, you may believe that falling in love is all dancing in the rain. I came of age in the era of Céline Dion, and my expectations were that near or far my heart would go on. For me, love was a ghost driving a motorcycle into my bedroom? For many generations, the idea of romantic love has been that your worlds revolve around one another. It's not love unless this person is everything to you, and you to them. Well, nothing helps you chill like realizing you will never be the most important person in your new partner's life. Aiming for a silver medal *at best* takes so much pressure off the situation for both of you. You don't need to be this person's everything because they already have a rich, full life outside of you. They have other people in their life—small people who may not yet know how to wipe their own butts—and those small people will *always* come before you. This is good for you! Because you'll realize that having a relationship doesn't mean sacrificing everything you enjoy at the altar of love. It means adding something great to your already awesome life. Rich and full seems like a way to describe coffee, or wine, so imagine your life as a cup of wine or coffee. When you're one hundred percent obsessed with your romantic partner, you become like a cup of hotel coffee: lukewarm, bitter, and a waste of time and resources. Is that extreme? Good!

THEY'RE LOOKING OUT FOR EVERYONE. Is this milk okay? Do you smell gas? Do you think I need a helmet? Don't worry, a parent has already poured out the expired milk, called the gas company to come out and inspect *just in case,* and buckled a helmet under your chin with the exact amount of slack needed to keep you comfortable *and* secure. Oh, and your AAA membership has been renewed ahead of the expiration deadline.

THEY'LL FEED YOU. Anyone who has been responsible for a small person knows that snacks are key. They will always have a snack available on their person, be thinking about your next snack, or prepared to stop the car for a snack. Dinner is at a regular time every day. The fridge is perpetually stocked. If they know where to get the cheapest gallon of milk and where the closest Costco is, cue the violins. This is real romance.

Chapter Twelve

The Gift

I keep a fork in my jewelry box.

It's not a fancy fork, either. It's the kind of fork a guy buys in the cheapest set of cutlery money can buy. The kind of fork that bends under any kind of resistance.

I've had it since 2010. My first date with Aaron. He'd handed it to me in a jewelry box, sliding it across the table like a guy from a commercial for a jewelry store chain trying to surprise his wife of ten years with a diamond tennis bracelet.

"Just a little something," he shrugged, "to make up for my mistake."

A few days earlier, I had been working on a Sunday morning, at an ad agency in downtown Minneapolis. I was there to finish everything I should have from Monday to Friday, when I was too busy chatting online with my friends and procrastinating. Aaron and I had been exchanging text messages all morning, and I walked through downtown Minneapolis to my office, listening to music and waiting to feel my phone buzz. He was at brunch with friends. He asked me what I liked to eat on weekends.

Coffee cake with lots of sugar, I replied, sitting at my desk fiddling around with a PowerPoint, a*nd dark roast coffee with cream, the color of a paper bag.*

One hour later, the doorbell rang at the office. The building was a huge converted warehouse that had been renovated over the course of a few decades, and the result was somewhere between a nineties McMansion and an M. C. Escher drawing. The doorbell rang again, which meant that nobody on the first floor was in, or that they refused to get the door. Annoyed, I started my journey to the main entrance.

Aaron was wearing his Ray-Ban's, a button up, and a cardigan. His four-door VW Golf idled at the curb.

"Hello, my high-powered businesswoman," he called out as I opened the door, "I brought you some brunch."

I opened the lid of the coffee. It was the exact color of a paper bag.

"Perfect," I said, and took a sip.

"Can we go out on a date this week?" he asked me, and I nodded.

"Great. Go get your work done, slacker."

He got back in his car and left.

Had I even said thank you?

I was all the way back at my desk when I realized that no, I hadn't thanked him, only walked into my office as if I was routinely surprised at work on a Sunday by a handsome, thoughtful man. Back at my desk, I opened the box he'd handed me to find a perfect piece of sugary coffee cake.

Hey, I texted him, *you forgot to get me a fork.*

Sorry, he replied, *it won't happen again.*

I was so unaccustomed to men being wholeheartedly kind to me that I didn't know how to react other than with sarcasm.

Aaron taught me to expect kindness, and how to accept it. He was funny and often sarcastic, but also genuine and earnest. When Aaron died, I found a file he kept on his computer desktop of things he thought I would like. There were gift ideas and albums to send me, and stupid photos and memes that would make me laugh. Aaron was the kind of person who made coffee without being asked, who played with the ends of my hair while we watched movies, who kept every text message we had ever exchanged, including the embarrassing ones from when I was wasted at my friend's wedding asking things like "Do you wants to get married soon?!" Love is in these little things, in small acts of kindness, in the simple consideration of another person. Aaron was always considering me, keeping me top of mind. Our big love grew from a million tiny considerations of one another: How he slept with a hand on me, because he was too claustrophobic for my brand of snuggling. How he laid in bed with me until I fell asleep—even when he wasn't tired—because he knew I couldn't fall asleep without him. How we started and ended any day apart with a phone call.

He spent the last four years of his life finding ways to make me smile.

And so would Matthew, I could tell. I could tell because he had been through some *stuff*. And the way he had managed it . . . showed me who he was. On our first date, we talked about our marriages, and how they'd changed us. I *loved* being married to Aaron. I gave him a five-star Yelp review and two thumbs-up. Matthew's crumbling marriage had destroyed him and transformed him. He'd left that marriage and become Super Matthew. Each hour of the past five years of his life had revolved around his children and his job. He was a man of strict routine, dedicated to making sure the children were never picked up or dropped off late, that they always had snacks and balanced meals. (I often fed Ralph a bowl of cereal while we sat in bed together, but I left that detail out.) Even when his life was falling apart, he'd gotten to work early and stayed late, had gotten a promotion each year and managed to hide the ugly truth from all of his coworkers and from his children. He'd done all of this alone, just like I had. And he wasn't bitter, or angry. He was the kind of person who genuinely liked doing nice things for other people. Who spent weekends helping his parents clean their gutters, or helping his daughter with a craft project she found on YouTube. He was the kind of guy who would spend his life being nice to me, if I let him.

I just . . . really didn't want to let him.

I had never been an independent person. Since age fifteen, I'd spent maybe six months of my life without a serious boyfriend, stepping from one relationship to another like singlehood was lava. Sure, I'd bought a bigger house than I needed, and made up bedrooms for kids who didn't exist. But dreaming of growth, of expanding our team of two, was different from actually growing. I knew how to set up my own Apple TV now (you just . . . plug it in). In the immortal words of the prophets Simon & Garfunkel, I was a rock, I was an island. It had taken me a year to become this self-sufficient machine, handling daycare drop-off and pick-up, work, mortgage payments, and dinner duty all on my own. I didn't want to let this kind-eyed man into my heart and my home, where he would most certainly fill the dishwasher without being asked, or shovel my walk when it snowed. I didn't want to accept any kindness, or owe any kindness.

Except, I kind of did, because the morning after my first date with Matthew, I did something very chill.

I went to a bookstore and bought a Moleskine notebook. And I wrote Matthew a card.

I told him that I'd woken up thinking about him, and everything he had been through in the past five years. I told him that I could see what he didn't: that he had kept his broken world together for his children, and that it was harder than it looked. I told him I was sorry he had been betrayed and broken, and that I was happy to be a person who benefited from his pain. Here is a notebook, I explained, I think you should write it all down, so you can look back and see what I see.

I had these items couriered to his office in downtown Minneapolis.

And then, I waited.

Hours passed between the delivery and the text message I received, which I was sure would read:

You're very nice. Also, I think we should never see each other again.

I opened the message.

I just got your package. I don't know what to say.

Cue: heart sinking.

But wait! Another message arrives.

You already understand me more than anyone I know. My head is spinning. I really like you.

I liked him, too. I liked him too *much*. I liked the dumb little space between his front teeth, and the way he fought the curl in his hair, always pushing it to the side as he talked. I liked his smile and I liked his voice. I liked that he had suffered and survived. I hated how much I liked him. I didn't want to get used to him, or love him, or need him. Because here is one thing that all human men have in common: stupid mortal bodies that will definitely die. I knew Matthew had smoked, so, obviously, there were already pre-cancerous cells floating around in his body, just waiting to gather together and take over, turning him from dark and handsome to ashen and dead. I knew Matthew had a car, so, obviously, it was only a matter of time before he crashed it, maybe even with me inside, leaving Ralph an orphan. I knew Matthew was alive, and it was only a matter of time until he was not. I also knew that all of this was so cliché I could barely stand to think about it. *Really, Nora? You're so afraid of losing again that you can't love? This is exactly the plot of every terrible made-for-TV movie. You're better than this! Be afraid of something more sensible! Like an invisible hand grabbing your ankle while you walk up the basement stairs!*

Matthew and his stupid, mortal body came over that night, after Ralph fell asleep.

"Can I read you a poem?" I asked as I handed him a glass of wine.

The correct answer to this question is "please do not," but Matthew said "sure," and sat on the couch while I sat cross-legged in front of the fireplace and cracked open Mary Oliver's book of poetry about her dead wife.

Love still as once you loved, deeply
and without patience. Let God and the world
know you are grateful. That the gift has been given.

I choked out those words from Mary's poem "The Gift," and stared at Matthew like, "do you *fully get* how weird and damaged I am?" His eyes betrayed no signs of terror, so I kept going. More Mary Oliver poems, coming right up!

I read and wept, and Matthew, who by this point should have definitely slipped quietly out my front door and blocked me from his contacts, stayed. Relax, he didn't stay the *night*. It was the second date. Is it a date if you just read a man poetry and weep while he sits on your couch? It is to me! Date or not, Matthew stayed until I fell asleep, driving clear across town and texting me "Home. Thank you for tonight. I can't wait to see you again."

He did wait, because we are adults with responsibilities. He came back the next week. And I let him.

Unexpected goodness is as large and overwhelming as unexpected tragedy. It feels as if all unexpected life events blow in all at once, like a summer storm that drops rocks of ice on your lawn on an eighty-degree day. That's true of the hard things: they arrive with an exclamation mark, sudden and declarative. But the good things are different. Looking back, you always see that they took their time. A high school boyfriend of mine told me that it's absolutely possible to be struck by lightning twice. He knew because it happened (twice!) to his uncle. It seemed impossible to me when he told me, but it doesn't anymore. If something extraordinary happens to you, why shouldn't it happen twice? Be just as likely to happen again? Why should I be surprised to find myself here? Why *shouldn't* I be feeling this electric rush of new love? I don't know how electricity works, and I'm thirty-five and not likely to become an electricity enthusiast at this age.

But I know that being loved really well made me more attuned to love itself. In my early twenties, I couldn't tell the difference between love and guys who were barely interested in me. I thought love could be born out of persistence, that given the right circumstances and the right amount of weed and alcohol, I could certainly convince a guy to love me. Aaron took no convincing, no persuading.

Loving him, and being loved by him, was easy. I had the good stuff with Aaron, and I lost it. But I didn't lose the muscle memory for it. I know what it is when I see it. I can meet a couple and quickly sense whether or not they're built to last, which sounds extremely judgmental (and absolutely is), but is also true.

I had the good stuff, and now I have the good sense not to let it sneak by me if I find it again. It's luck, but it's not as random as lightning, which, it turns out, isn't even random. It's all about ions and electrical charges. About the reaction of energies to one another. I just told you I'm not at an age where I'm going to learn much about electricity, but I did a cursory Google and the National Severe Storms Laboratory has a very instructional page titled "Lightning 101."

They confirmed my high school boyfriend's observation that lightning can absolutely strike twice in the same place. Maybe just as a fluke, but perhaps, also, because there is some quality about the location that makes it more likely to be struck.

This lightning struck because I was ready for it—I was basically standing in the rain, wrapped with tinfoil, using a plugged-in hair dryer. I knew a good thing when I saw it, because I'd had a good thing before. The gift had been given.

Chapter Thirteen

Too Soon

Love is strange. You won't find that in the Bible, but they should update 1 Corinthians to reflect that.

Love is patient

Love is kind

Love is absolutely bizarro.

I love love. But it makes no sense that we can smell someone's terrible breath every morning and still want to spend our lives with them. It is completely bonkers that after we've had our heart put through a meat grinder, we just gather up the chunks and say, "Well, let's try again!"

Love is universally regarded as the highest thing that we can strive for, as something not only worth pursuing, but worth fighting for, worth *dying* for if you're into that. And the strangest thing about love is that we have opinions about love that isn't ours. I do. You do. We all do. Because baseball is criminally boring, our national pastime is to analyze the relationships of others: celebrities, friends, absolute strangers who post annoying Instagram photos. Love is entertainment. Love is sport.

My father used to tell me that the only people who knew anything about a relationship were the two people who were in it. Anybody else's commentary was pure speculation, baseless opinion. But I *love* baseless opinion! I *love* reading articles where a relationship expert analyzes photos of celebrity couples and deciphers their relationship via body language. I *love* looking at a couple's wedding album and guessing how long it will take them to file for divorce. I am an absolute jerk!

And *that's* why I didn't want anyone to know about Matthew. Matthew is a handsome man with olive skin and giant blue eyes and dark, curly hair. He has a "strong" nose, which, because everyone secretly wants to date their dad, is always an essential for me. Even his *hands* are good-looking, and still, I hid him away like the hunchback of Notre Dame. I didn't make him live in a tower, mainly because he did have children to raise and a job to go to, I just . . . didn't really go out in public with him. Aside from Costco and the occasional movie, our relationship developed via FaceTime, text messages, and the two nights a week where he didn't have his children and Ralph had gone to sleep. It didn't feel like a conscious choice I was making, it felt like the natural development of a relationship between two parents with limited time to share with each other. Of *course*, most of our time together would be on my couch. But even on nights when we had a babysitter, we'd end up at restaurants in parts of town I never went to, or in movie theaters in the suburbs. Or in Costco. I was not joking about Costco.

One night, Matthew met me for a drink after a funeral for a friend's husband. I could have invited him *to* the funeral, which is a pretty good date spot, but I didn't. I had him meet me afterward at the downstairs bar. I regretted it immediately. I could tell that some of the funeral attendees had the same idea I did, not about the dating but about the drinking, and felt myself waiting to feel their eyes on me. And then it happened. A hand on my shoulder. A friend of a friend who used to work with Aaron. I couldn't remember her name, but I pretended to know exactly who she was. Normally, when I can't remember someone's name, I turn to the person I'm with and introduce *them*. That's what normal people do. Instead, I just faked my way through some small talk, and turned myself to face her, as if Matthew were a perfect stranger I'd been seated next to randomly. When she moved on, to a table in the back, I turned back to the bar, though not toward Matthew. We made eye contact in the mirror behind the bar, and he smiled.

I prepared an explanation in my head, a lie, of course. About how I had simply forgotten to introduce him, how I always do that, it's nothing personal. But I didn't have to lie to him. I thought immediately about the plaque hanging in the living room of my son's daycare provider.

Never explain yourself
The people who love you don't need it
The people who don't will never believe you anyway.

Matthew didn't need an explanation, and the weight of the moment slid from my shoulders. I didn't need to lie. I didn't need to explain. He got it. He got *me*. Matthew smoothed out some bills and placed them under his glass, catching the eye of the bartender as he stood up.

"I'm sorry about that," I said, still only looking into the mirror.

"I know," he replied. Matthew instinctively knew how to love me, just like Aaron had. It isn't the same love, and they aren't the same men. Aaron and Matthew are very different people. Aaron was tall and outgoing, the sort of magnetic person who shined a bright, warm light of inclusion on anyone he touched. I was "Aaron's girlfriend," and he was the star of the show. I loved that dynamic. I loved watching him shine. I loved that he could stand up in front of a crowd of strangers and do a theatrical rendition of a Céline Dion duet while I watched from the audience, laughing along. I admired him, and the way he could command the attention of an entire room of drunk people who could barely focus their eyes. When we met, I had a hard time standing up in front of a room full of my own colleagues to talk about my own ideas without spontaneously combusting. This surprises people who know me now, people who have seen me step on stage in front of a thousand people or listened to my podcast. And the only explanation I can come up with is that I took on some of Aaron's unselfconsciousness by osmosis. Slowly, at first, through our relationship, with the balance being directly transferred to me upon his death.

Matthew is so shy that I think if a scientist offered him the opportunity to grow a turtle shell that he could pop into whenever he found himself in an overwhelming social situation, which by his definition is anything with more than two people in attendance, he would take it. He has one flaw, and that is his insistence that he is five-eleven, even though he is clearly five-ten. I only bring this up because I think he lied about his height on his driver's license and if there is anyone reading this who works for the Minnesota Department of Vehicle Services, please contact me immediately so we can resolve this important legal issue.

Aaron and Matthew are different, but we fell into sync the same way. We met, and we were together.

When Matthew and I met, I was open to love *theoretically*. Thinking about what I wanted was easy. Finding what I wanted was surprisingly easy. Enjoying what I wanted? Basically impossible. It had been when I found Aaron, too. On our second date, Aaron told me that he had just come off a decade-long relationship with the only serious girlfriend he'd had besides me. He was freshly single, and I told him to his face that I was not interested in dating him until he had taken his time. Anyone could objectively look at him and say it was just too soon to be dating someone new.

I didn't know anything about his previous relationship, but I had a swift opinion about what should happen next. Behavior post-relationship falls into two camps. For women it goes this way. Date too soon after your relationship ends, and you're just rebounding. Take too long and you're dwelling on the past. But for men, these judgments are a little softer. Rushing into a relationship shows a certain softness that ladies can't resist, and avoiding commitment makes you a desirable bachelor. For women, we are always walking the tightrope between being a floozy or an old maid. Another check in our column, am I right?

There is no standard prescription for what to do when you've lost love. If there were, I would have hoarded up bottles of it before my husband died, and I wouldn't have been sitting at a bar pretending not to know a man who had most definitely seen me naked.

I told myself that I was sparing Matthew the judgment of others. If people were as harsh as I was, then everyone—including that stranger at the bar—would think it was just *too soon*. But the harshest judgment I felt was from me. If I loved Aaron, what was I doing falling in love with this guy? If I was still so bone-achingly sad about Aaron's death, why was I so comforted by the feeling of Matthew's hands on my bare skin? There is a difference between guilt and shame. Guilt says *I did something bad* and shame says *I am bad*. I had both, swirled together like a really awful twist cone. *It* was bad to fall in love with someone new, because I was still in love with Aaron. *I* was bad to fall in love with someone new, because it meant I couldn't love Aaron. It was all bad. I didn't need anyone to tell me what they thought. It was hard enough to deal with my own brain.

I did what any mature person would do when she finds herself the meat in a guilt and shame sandwich: I booked a flight to the other side of the country. I ran away. Not *just* because of Matthew, but because of Aaron. His deathaversary was coming, and the entire city of Minneapolis felt haunted and raw. I didn't know what I would do on November 25, only that I couldn't do it in the city where we'd fallen in love, the city where he'd died.

I fled to a city where Aaron and I had never traveled together. Somewhere roughly seventy degrees warmer than Minneapolis in November. Ralph and I spent Aaron's first deathaversary at my friend Tyler's house in Hollywood. If that sounds like I'm trying to brag and impress you, I completely am. Tyler and his wife would be out of town that weekend, and they offered us their very nice, very kid-free home for us to just hang out and do whatever it is you do to commemorate a monumental loss in your lives. I'd spent a year thinking about this day, and what it would mean to me. The first year after Aaron's death was filled with a million firsts, but this would be the biggest one. Something would happen, I was sure. I would feel different, be different. I would mark this day with something meaningful. A thousand balloons released into the sky (not eco-friendly). A lantern released into the sky (not safe in dry, brittle California). There had to be some kind of meaningful ceremony I could throw together on the fly after wasting an entire year of planning time!

Indeed there was. At the moment Aaron's death became officially one year old, Ralph and I were splitting a gluten-free pizza. We raised our glasses and had a toast.

"To Papa," I said. "To Papa!" Ralph cheered. And then it was time for his afternoon nap.

When Aaron died, the first person I called was . . . Aaron. He was the person I called when anything big happened, and nothing was bigger than his death. Moe and I had taken that place for one another when we met. We didn't have Andy and Aaron anymore, so we became each other's First Call. Moe was the only person who remembered to call me on Aaron's deathaversary. Andrew's had just passed, and we'd laid in her bed together on that day. I remember her telling me that the day hadn't hurt more than any other, that the anticipation of it was worse than its arrival.

When I left town, I told Matthew not to expect to hear from me. I liked him and all, but this was a special and sacred time for me and I couldn't be distracted by him. He wasn't to call me or text me. And he didn't.

But I wanted him to. I wanted to tell him about this day, about how it hadn't hurt as much as I thought it would, and how that scared me. About how Ralph had invented a little brother named Gary and would make me pretend to buckle both of them into car seats and kiss them both good night. I wanted him to know that Ralph had sat on the deck with me and watched the sun set, and then asked me to howl like a wolf with him. I wanted him to know these things, I wanted him to know that I didn't know how to feel, about time, and memories, about the future, about the past colliding with the present, about him. About anything.

He picked up after one ring.

Chapter Fourteen

Not *That* Kind of Christian

Mom, please skip this chapter because you aren't going
to like what I have to say, and I really love your waffles.

To say that God and I have had a rocky relationship would be an exaggeration, mainly because we didn't really *have* a relationship. I imagine this will be disappointing for my mother after paying for eighteen years of Catholic education, but repetition and memorization is not a form of connection.

I knew the Lord's Prayer, the Hail Mary, and could fake my way through the Apostle's Creed, but the moment I stepped into church, my brain took a short vacation and my body took over. Sit. Stand. Sit. Stand. Sit. St-shit . . . no. Kneel? If you keep your eyes open and move your mouth enough, nobody will know that you have no idea what's going on. I feared, as a child, that I was the only one who felt this way. That all around me were devout Catholics who found meaning in the reading of the Gospel according to That One Guy. Who could follow along with Father Whatshisface's homily. That I was the only one who spent those sixty minutes trying to count the number of panels in each stained-glass window. I knew there must be some reason why our parents brought us here every week. Maybe I had missed it. If it were important enough for us to spend an hour a week here, all of this must mean something, but I didn't feel *anything*. The words—and whatever they meant—just slid off me, like oil. After communion, my family and I would slip on our coats and slip out the side door and back into our normal lives, having crossed Religion off our to-do list. Religion was a thing we did, once a week. Like taking out the trash or ordering pizza.

All of this pains my mother, I know. She and my father both grew up Catholic, in a South Minneapolis neighborhood where each three-bedroom house was home to at least six children per family. Being Catholic wasn't a choice for them, it was a cultural expectation. In second grade, all the children had their first communion, dressing up like tiny brides and grooms for their first taste of the body and blood of Christ. Shortly after, they'd have their first confessions, sliding into a dark booth to recite their childish sins to a man who could offer them a chore list of prayers meant to earn the forgiveness of God. And in high school, they'd been confirmed into the faith, which is basically signing a contract that says, "Yeah, I've looked over the purchase agreement, and this all looks great to me. Sign me up for a lifetime of Catholicism." My parents had both done all these things, and baptized each of their babies into the faith, but I didn't know why, and I never thought to ask. I assumed that whatever it meant to them had to have been explained to me at some time, and I wasn't listening. And what kind of an idiot child needs to have religion explained to her? I certainly wasn't bold enough, or confident enough, to raise my hand in a Cathedral with saints looming above my head and say, "Wait, what is this all about?"

Even if I'd asked these big questions, I don't know that the people around me would have been able to clarify. Sometimes, the appeal of Catholicism seemed to be in the difficulty people had in understanding it. The bread and wine we took at communion wasn't symbolic, it was *actually* the body and blood of Christ. It's called transubstantiation, and it happens after the consecration, and you'll need to look up both those words on your own. Even the structure of the organization felt complicated: the main boss is the pope, but there are cardinals and archbishops and bishops and priests and brothers and nuns, and they are all the boss of their own little area? I never got an org chart. The complication of it all seemed intentional: a way to make it seem more mysterious, but also more intellectual. The beauty is that it's hard to understand, like *Game of Thrones* or *True Detective*, and if you need it explained to you, well, then I guess you aren't cool enough to get it. Maybe?

I COULDN'T UNDERSTAND WHY ONLY men could lead a church, why the death penalty was okay but murder was wrong, why abortion was just as bad as birth control, or why our parish priest had shrugged it off when my middle school friend ran to him in desperation when his stepfather began viciously beating his mother. Jesus seemed pretty cool, but all the stuff around him felt like some real bull crap.

Generations of McInernys and Farleys had signed up for this club. Surely there was a reason why they stayed, even when it became clear the barrier to entry wasn't high enough. Was the driving force simply the fact that it's what generations of McInernys and Farleys had always done? If religion *did* mean something to my parents—really *meant* something—I never heard about it.

And then Aaron happened. We were together for a year before his brain tumor showed up. We were young and stupid and in the phase of love where everything you read reminds you of the other person, especially a quote from a long-dead writer about the ill-fated love of his life.

> I love her, and that's the beginning and the end
> of everything. You're still a Catholic, but Zelda's the
> only God I have left now.
> —F. SCOTT FITZGERALD

My pretend Catholicism was over. I didn't have an hour to spend zoning out in some uncomfortable pews. I didn't have time to do anything except Aaron. Shut up, you know what I mean. Aaron was the only God I had left, but suddenly, everyone was pushing *God* like it was a hot new drug that could get me high enough to pretend my perfect boyfriend hadn't just been diagnosed with an aggressive and incurable brain cancer. In the absence of those creature comforts of predictability and a firm and stable plot line to our lives, it's our reflex to want to invoke the name of God. God may not make sense, but at least God is predictable in her unpredictability. It's God who gives you what you can handle, and only what you can handle. It's God who planned this, so it's pointless for you to worry about it. It's God who will see you through, even though it's also God who planned this? The religious platitudes were heaped upon me like so many Midwestern Hot Dishes, and I would have none of them. God had not done this. "What does God have to do with this?" I wanted to shout at every person who tweeted their #thoughtsandprayers to me while Aaron's body wasted next to me. What does a prayer do? What kind of a God is listening, but not doing anything? I envied people who could believe like this, and I resented them for assuming that my own discomfort could be eased with the same balm that soothed them when our pain was so different. Not to their faces, of course. I smiled and thanked them, told them to keep on praying, told them how much I appreciated it.

Narrator: she did not appreciate it.

God would not stop this. But I could. I could save Aaron. Maybe not medically—he had stage-four brain cancer and I had tragically chosen to major in English instead of something useful—but in every way that I possibly could, I would make his life better. I would make him organic, fresh-pressed juice every day even when he just wanted a Mountain Dew. I would marry him. Have his baby. Scratch his back while he fell asleep at night, noticing each night how more vertebrae pushed toward his skin. Our family didn't need God. We had each other. And we had a community of people who showed up when God had failed to. People showed up to mow our lawn. To shovel our walk. To paint our basement. To drive us to chemo and radiation, or to watch our child so we could do these things without him. They fundraised for Aaron's medical bills. They brought us hot dishes. They packed a huge art gallery for his funeral.

MY FRIEND KYLEE IS A CHRISTIAN. Like a *Christian* Christian. The kind who goes to church and reads the Bible. I knew that when we met—about a year after Aaron died—but I decided to let it slide. We had followed each other on Instagram for some time, and while a few of her posts were about Jesus stuff, most of them were about her photography and video work, her kid, and the creative circle of women she runs with here in Minneapolis. Kylee never told me that Aaron's death was a part of God's plan, or told me I needed to pray more. She never told me I needed to pray at all.

God was a part of Kylee's life in a way I hadn't really witnessed before. Not as an all-knowing, all-seeing Father who had a blueprint for your life, who you had to beg for forgiveness or for help, but as a calm center inside of her. Once, over lunch at the kind of place where everything is organic and grown within ten miles of the table you're sitting at, I asked her how she prays. She laughed and shrugged. "I don't know, I just . . . talk?"

You just . . . *talk*? Don't you have something to memorize?

Sometimes, she explained, she pictured God as an ocean. Standing on the edge, she could throw in her worries, and watch them be swept out to sea. I liked that.

After lunch, having scraped our leftovers into the compost bin and placed our dirty dishes in the bus bin, we hugged good-bye.

"You're being held in God's hands," she said to me as we pulled apart. It was very early in our friendship. Too early in our friendship, frankly, but for some reason I didn't want to sock her in the throat or block her number. I felt relieved. The months since Aaron died had been a never-ending treadmill of busyness and accomplishment. I'd quit my job, and racked up freelance clients. I'd written my first book and started a nonprofit. I shuttled Ralph from daycare to gymnastics to whatever else it felt like a good mother would take him to. It was all on me, I knew. Or I thought.

After our lunch, I sat in my car and cried. The car is actually one of my favorite places to cry, because it's like a little semiprivate pod where you feel invisible enough to really let loose, even though anybody with vision can see exactly what you're up to.

Since that day with Kylee, I have relived the years I had spent with Aaron, and I have started to see them differently, the way Kylee saw them that day outside the restaurant. I saw how unfair it was that Aaron was sick, and how lucky we were to be caught in the middle of our freefall and held up. That is not the blessing that everyone gets when their lives fall apart. There are plenty of people who suffer alone, or whose social circles don't have the means to build them a safety net to fall into. But we were never alone, and we never hit the ground. We were made safer and seen through the hardest parts of our lives. I had been so angry about what God hadn't done that I'd missed everything that people *had* done for us. People fed us and cared for us. They paid our bills. Some of these were our friends and family, but most of the people who reached out to help us were strangers. People who had never met us, and likely never will. They didn't do it for a thank-you note or for a few extra karma points. They did it because we needed their help, and they had help to give.

They showed up, and they brought God with them. Because God, to me, is just people. It's that simple, and it's that hard. God is people. God is the best of them, and the worst of them. And the path to God does not start in a Church. It doesn't even need to wind through one. You have a direct line to God, and you don't need to make a Sunday appointment to see Her. God is here, whether you like her or not. Whether you need her or not. Whether or not you believe in her. That there is no magic spell to invoke, no special code to learn, no door that must be opened to you.

You are the code and the secret and the door. You are God. Don't get a big head about it, though.

Chapter Fifteen

Flip the Nuggets

There were places I couldn't go with Matthew, places that still belonged to Aaron, and maybe always will. Northeast Minneapolis—where Aaron and I lived—was off-limits. Live music—a regular night out for me and Aaron—was a no-go. And he couldn't—wouldn't—meet Ralph. Ralph wasn't just *mine*; he was *ours*. Mine and Aaron's. Ralph wouldn't meet a man until we'd been together for years. No, he'd never meet a man! I'd live my life completely separately from any man I met. I'd be a dedicated mom with a sidepiece who understood that my life revolved around one small person. It would be terribly modern. Matthew agreed. He had kids, too, after all. They'd already endured a dramatic divorce. They didn't need to get all attached to a woman who only wanted their father around as a male concubine. The rules were set in my living room, with the fireplace roaring and Ralph asleep upstairs. Across town, Matthew's children were asleep at their other home. It was like a business deal, only made cross-legged on my floor, drinking wine from old jelly jars.

"Not for at least six months," Matthew said, and raised his glass for a toast. I clinked my glass with his. This would be over in less than six months, of course. It *was* best if we always kept those parts of our lives separate.

I knew lots of widows who pulled this off: whose boyfriends or girlfriends came over after bedtime and left before dawn. We did this for weeks. Six weeks, to be exact. I saw Matthew only those nights when his kids were at their other home. I was careful not to text him during his parent time, so as not to raise suspicion between Ian and Sophie. Ralph had become the kind of toddler who reliably slept through the night, in his own bed, and Matthew would wake up hours before Ralph, and head home to get ready for work. I slept deeply and peacefully with him beside me. On my bedside table, he'd leave a note and a cup of coffee with the perfect amount of cream. If it had snowed, he'd shovel the walkway and steps before he left.

I resisted all of these kindnesses.

"You don't have to do that," I'd say, halfway between annoyed and grateful, when he took the groceries from the back of my car.

"I know," he said, "but I want to do it."

Matthew and Ralph met accidentally, a slip of our spy-like, stealthy dating. Matthew arrived a few minutes early to pick me up, and Ralph was procrastinating his bedtime routine for a babysitter. It was . . . anticlimactic. Ralph could not have been less interested in meeting Matthew. Ralph knew a lot of adults—he had a whole stable of babysitters to pick him up from daycare, take him to fancy toy stores—so one more grown-up was nothing to him, especially if they were just hanging out in the living room playing LEGO. What I assumed would be a monumental event was nothing to this child. Maybe (definitely) I was making more out of this than I needed to.

Not to say that Ralph needed to be flipping through Tinder looking for his next Father Figure, but maybe I could just let life happen?

Here's how life happened: Ralph got to know Matthew slowly, ten or fifteen minutes at a time. He asked questions like "Do you have boys?," which really meant "Do you have kids?" and Matthew nodded. "I have a boy, and a girl. Ian and Sophie." All Ralph heard was boy, and every time he saw Matthew, he asked where "The Boys" were.

We'd talked a lot about Matthew's kids. I knew how their extracurricular activities were going, and what their report cards said. But I'd never met them. I didn't know if I was *qualified* to meet them. I had been eighteen when Ian was born, didn't that make me basically his peer? Sophie was my niece's friend—wouldn't that be weird for them? And both Ian and Sophie were old enough to understand what a girlfriend was. Would they feel uncomfortable knowing their dad was kissing someone on the mouth? Would they feel their little team of three was being infringed upon? Would they meet me, immediately scream "You're not my mother!" and storm away?

I didn't want to get involved in their lives if we weren't sure about one another, but I couldn't be sure about this man without knowing him as a dad. Being a dad is a huge part of Matthew's identity. Not just because he has kids, but because he *acts* like he has them. We all know a guy who is "technically" a parent. Sure, he loves his kids, but it also seems like he kinda got tricked into the whole situation. A guy who refers to spending time with his kids as "babysitting" or who idealizes his glory days of being young and single. Matthew is the opposite of that guy. Knowing nothing about him, you could spot Matthew on the street and *know* he's a dad. He doesn't wear cargo pants or Teva sandals (thank God), but he exudes a paternal air, like he is constantly ready to cut someone's meat into nonchokable pieces or secure a car seat correctly. I kid you not, he keeps a nail clipper on him *at all times*. His default mode of speaking is a Dad Voice that urges you, in its tone and timbre, to listen carefully. After his divorce, Matthew spent any evening without his children sitting at work until it was time to go to bed. That way, he explained to me, he didn't have time to miss them. On the flip side, I would often lock the bathroom door just so I could read in peace, and scream in terror when Ralph slid his fingers under the door, groping around for my toes.

We decided to not make a big deal of the whole meet-the-kids thing. It was nearly Christmas, so the plan became that we would all meet up on a weekend afternoon to make Christmas cookies and watch a Christmas movie. We would not touch or kiss in front of the kids; we'd just act like old friends that our kids had never happened to meet before this day.

Ralph watched out the window for hours until Matthew pulled into the driveway with The Boys. Ian, fourteen, looked tiny and frightened in the front seat. Sophie, nine, bounded out of the back-seat wearing a puffy, purple winter coat and a floor-length tulle skirt over her winter boots. She stepped in the front door, beaming, and asked where the kitchen was. Ralph ran to Ian, hugging his knees, and Ian broke into a huge smile. He took Ralph's little hand, and got tugged along into the living room to look at a Star Wars book. So far, so good. I shook Matthew's hand.

The afternoon stretched into evening. We made puppy chow and peanut butter kisses and decorated sugar cookies. Ralph asked to show Ian and Sophie his Motorcycle Room, the empty basement where I let him ride his bike in circles. The Boys showed Ralph how to kick a soccer ball, and took turns helping him on his balance bike. Sophie unrolled the gymnastics mat and challenged me to a head-stand contest, which I promptly lost. Matthew's children were sweet and kind to Ralph, and Ralph was effervescent with joy at the presence of other kids in his house.

Dinner was a culinary masterpiece of chicken nuggets and tater tots, which Matthew took charge of. My preparation of this meal includes the following steps:

1. Rip open each bag however you can. I prefer to dig a fingernail right into the center of the bag, and open from there.

2. Dump the contents onto a baking sheet, and kinda spread them around.

3. Put the baking sheets into the oven and forget until you smell something subtly burning.

Matthew had a different approach. I walked into the kitchen to find each of the nuggets equally spaced on a baking sheet, and the tater tots laid out the same way . . . on their own sheet? I watched skeptically. After ten minutes, an alarm sounded on Matthew's phone, and he reached for the oven. "They aren't done yet!" I shouted, like he was an imbecile. He looked at me and said, "It's time to flip the nuggets."

Flip. The. Nuggets? That is not on the instructions! "This way," he said, concentrating on keeping the perfect spacing between each artificially formed hunk of chicken by-product, "they're crispy on *both* sides."

Did these kids realize what kind of a father they had? A nugget-flipping angel who wanted them to enjoy perfectly crispy pieces of breaded chicken parts reconstituted into tasty, asymmetrical blobs? They did. Matthew doted on his children that evening in a way that made it clear this was not a onetime performance. He watched their glasses and filled them with water before they were empty. He handed them napkins before they even asked. And his kids looked at him like the perfect nugget-and-tot-making saint he was.

After dinner, The Boys asked if they could help Ralph get ready for bed. Matthew and I loaded the dishwasher and listened to them coaxing Ralph into brushing his teeth quickly, so he could watch part of *Home Alone* before he went to bed. They carried him downstairs with cozy PJs on and fresh breath, and he snuggled between them and pretended to follow the plot of a movie that wasn't a cartoon. When it was time for Ralph to go to bed, The Boys paused the movie and came upstairs to read Ralph his bedtime books and help tuck him in, and when I came back downstairs to finish the movie with them, I found Ian, Sophie, and Matthew snuggled up in a chair. A one-person armchair. Of all the seats in our cozy living room, a fourth grader and an eighth grader wanted to be jammed into a single chair with their dad, who gently played with the hair on each of their heads while they ate popcorn and laughed at the misfortune of the Wet Bandits. I was getting a sneak peek into who Matthew was as a dad, and as a person. That was it.

I was officially in love with this nugget-flipping, kid-cuddling, dad and a half. I wanted him in my life, and Ralph's life. I wanted to be in Ian and Sophie's life. I was in. Not for the modern, no-strings-attached kind of relationship I had imagined, but for the gorgeously mundane one we were having today. I was in for movies on the couch and off-brand chicken nuggets and playing soccer in the basement. It had only been a month, and I was in. All in. I was in love. And for some reason, I said it. I said it when we were both in the kitchen, dishing up bowls of popcorn. I didn't say the whole chicken nugget part, but I said the three most important words, the ones I was sure I'd never say again. I didn't realize I was going to say them until they were already out. Was I crazy? I was crazy. But Matthew smiled at me right away.

"Thank you," he said, and left the room. "Okaaaaaay," I thought, "that is a fair response and I will not take it personally. It is unfair of me to assume that he should reciprocate my feelings on my schedule."

That's what my brain said. But as soon as the kids clamored upstairs to check on Ralphie, I leaned into him on the couch and let my heart take over.

"Did you hear me back there?" I whispered. "I said I love you."

He turned to look me in the eye.

"I heard you," he said. "I was just surprised. I love you, too."

I kissed him, quickly, in case the kids had developed X-ray vision that could penetrate the floor above us.

"Good," I said.

Chapter Sixteen

Meet the Parents
(All of Them)

My father always told my boyfriends "you marry a person, you marry their family." It was his way of making sure these guys knew that the McInernys are a package deal, and that should they choose to marry me, they'd be committing to a family that still practices the ancient art of Tickle Torture. It is one of many traditions within the McInerny family that may be considered child abuse, but one person is attacked by the rest of the family and tickled mercilessly right up to the brink of peeing their pants. It's great fun unless you're the person trying not to pee your pants, but even then, it does feel nice to be the center of attention.

Matthew didn't get to meet my dad, which is a tragedy because my dad would have had so much fun with him. Not *with* him actually, but with making fun of him in his presence. My dad loved making fun of vegetarians, Wisconsinites, and anyone who dated me, making Matthew a perfect trifecta for mockery. Matthew had grown up in small-town Wisconsin, a state that brags about having the most bars per capita. He'd briefly attended the University of Wisconsin, which has a sports rivalry with the University of Minnesota, which my father attended. Neither Matthew nor my dead dad particularly care for sports, but a rivalry is a rivalry, I suppose. After dropping out of college, which my father had also done, Matthew moved to the Big City: Minneapolis. He lived in dilapidated houses with too many other boys his age, played drums in bands I have never heard of, and, surrounded by punk vegetarians, swore off meat when he was eighteen years old. Not for any reasons surrounding humane treatment of animals, but mainly just to fit in. My dad would have had a field day with this guy.

"Oh, great, a *vegetarian*. You want my wife to make you a mushroom steak? Maybe that's how they do things in *Wisconsin*, but not here, pal."

"Nora, can you kindly explain to your friend from Wisconsin that we remove our shoes before entering a person's home? Was he born in a barn?"

"Matthew, would you like a cup of coffee? Is cream okay? Or is that not *vegetarian*?"

All of these things make my dad sound like some kind of meathead, when really, he was just a geek who liked crossword puzzles and Anthony Trollope and whose love language was mockery.

So, Matthew never got to be roasted by my dad. Instead, he got the next best thing: meeting my entire family all at once, during Sunday brunch. These are a regular thing for our family. Brunch is easier than trying to arrange dinner with a bunch of little kids with early bedtimes and too many activities. Plus, brunch tastes better. It's mainly sugar. My mother typically hosts, and provides the waffles and coffee. My siblings and I provide . . . nothing, really. We show up, with our hungry, crabby kids, and let them run wild through our mom's house while we all catch up at the dining room table. If you're expecting a big scene wherein my family is overly protective of their widowed sister, and really puts her potential mate through the wringer in order to test his mettle? Well, be prepared to be as disappointed as I was, because they welcomed Matthew into the McInerny fold as if he had always been there. In other words, they treated him like he was nothing special. My mother's first feedback about Matthew was that we already have a Matthew in the family, and would need to call him something else. I suggested Matty, but she claimed that she sometimes called her brother that, which I had never actually heard her do, but I let it slide. Eventually, Matthew was renamed Marty against his will, because an uncle we barely ever see shares the same name as millions of adult men in America. Matthew had been a vegetarian for eighteen years, but my mother put a plate of bacon in front of him anyway, and eventually, he caved and ate a piece. She makes very good bacon and is a very persuasive presence when it comes to salty breakfast meats, and most things if I'm being honest.

Before this brunch, when we had been dating a few weeks, we were wandering the aisles of Costco looking for a particular kind of sock Matthew swears by when he asked me if I wanted to meet his parents.

"Sure," I said, trying to decide if the twenty-pack of full-butt-coverage underwear was a good deal.

"They live five minutes away," he replied, and I realized he meant "Do you want to meet my parents in five minutes."

My answer was still "sure," even though I hadn't washed my hair in several days and had slept in the yoga pants I was wearing. Meeting the parents last minute? I live for this shit. Matthew's mother, Shari, does not live for this shit. She does not enjoy a drop-in from her beloved son and the only lady friend they've met since his divorce on a November Saturday while she's sorting through Christmas decorations. She answered the door and went into complete shock, as if I had presented her with Matthew's severed head. "You're . . . you're very tall," she said, and immediately and endlessly apologized for her messy house. It was the cleanest house I had ever been in, but I forgave her anyway because that's the kind of person I am. In the hour or so I spent on their couch, Jim and Shari gave me a very convincing pitch for Matthew. Did I know he was the valedictorian of his college class? That he gave a commencement speech? They had taped it, and they could probably find it somewhere. Did I know that Matthew had walked at nine months old? That he was the best dad *they had ever seen*? I had just watched this man do a price comparison of peanut butter in Costco, but this endorsement made his stock soar. This *was* a good guy. I left their house with a full heart, and with a bottle of Perrier for the road. Matthew's mom and dad even walked us out to the car and hugged us each good-bye.

A few weeks later, he met my whole family, got his new nickname, and that was it. We'd met the parents. It was a lock. But we hadn't met *all* of the parents.

I married Aaron knowing I was marrying his family, just like he was marrying mine. We would go to dinner with our parents regularly, and Aaron and my brothers hung out without me often enough that it sometimes hurt my feelings because I like Marvel movies, too, okay?

After the funeral, though, Aaron's death settled in between me and everyone I considered family. None of us knew what to do with this expansive sadness, but the gulf was biggest between me and Kim, Aaron's mother. We still saw one another, we still loved one another, but we couldn't do the grief together.

Even if you're surrounded by people you love, figuring out grief is a solo project. Aaron was loved by many, and was a loss to many.

But he was (to my knowledge) only *my* husband. And (STET) he was Kim's only son.

Kim is the illustration of the perfect mother-in-law. Her nails and lips are always red. Her voicemails are, at a minimum, ninety seconds long. She will not send a text message without a heart emoji or an *xoxo*. She remembers to send a card for every holiday, and she always, always leaves any home tidier than she found it. From the day we met, I loved her, and I loved how much she loved Aaron, which was different from how most of my boyfriend's moms had loved them, which was for some reason always borderline romantic, and made me feel like the other woman. I love a mama's boy, but I don't want to compete with my boy's mama, ya know?

Most of my friends have really great stories about their nightmarish mothers-in-law, and I do someday plan on being that MIL to whomever my children marry, but Kim is and always was just . . . wonderful. Which does not make for good stories, as you can tell. "My mother-in-law is always so good to me!" doesn't have the same intrigue as "My mother-in-law once brought our toddler as a third wheel on a Match.com date when she was supposed to take him to music class."

I'd married Aaron, and I'd married his whole family. We just didn't know how to be family without him.

There isn't really a guidebook out there called *How to Tell Your Mother-in-Law You Are Dating Again*. I would write one, but I am not qualified to do it because I didn't have to sit Kim down and tell her about Matthew. She did all the work for me. I was sitting on her couch in early December, waiting for Ralph to wake up from his nap in her guest room. She'd poured us each a drink, and we sat on the couch and gossiped. Gossiping with Kim makes me miss Aaron. Aaron was a great gossip—prolific, though never cruel—and just when she was getting to the good part of her story, she paused and switched topics.

"I just want you to know, that someday you're going to meet someone, and I know that. I hope you do. You're wonderful, and I love you. I just always want to be in your life."

She had been nervous to say this to me, I could tell. Not because her voice shook, or because she was fidgeting, but because the words came out in such a precise and measured way that I knew she had practiced it many times, had probably meant to bring it up to me for months. This realization crushed me. This was her reaching across the space that Aaron left. All I had to do was meet her halfway. I said all the right things. Of *course* she would always be in my life. Of *course* she would always be Ralph's Mae Mae.

I said *"of course"* but I knew why she had to say it out loud: because death is loss compounded. You lose your son, or your husband, and then what do you lose? More people. Lots of people. Not to death itself, but as the emotional aftermath. I'd lost people. Kim had lost people. And we'd almost lost one another.

I said *of course* and then I said *actually*. Actually, I had met someone. His name is Matthew.

"Matthew," she said, like it was a word she was learning for the first time. "And he's nice? Of course he's nice."

She had not had time to rehearse this part—the reaction—so our conversation stumbled and meandered. She was glad to hear I'd met him through Moe. She was glad to hear he was divorced, and a dad. Her second husband, who had helped her raise Aaron and his little sister, was also a divorced dad. They're a good choice. We were interrupted by Ralph, who had woken up from his nap and wandered into the living room, where the two women who love him the most on this planet were wiping tears from their eyes and holding hands.

Puffy-eyed and warm from sleep, still sucking his little thumb, he snuggled in between us both.

DATING ME IS A FORM of exposure therapy, in that you will be exposed to a lot of things that make you uncomfortable and will subsequently need therapy.

Say, for example, that I'm officiating my dead husband's best friend's wedding three months into our relationship: you're going to carpool to the ceremony with my toddler and my dead husband's mother. She'll pick you up around five if that's okay.

Matthew and Mae Mae had met briefly just before the wedding, but I thought that the forty-five-minute drive to the middle of nowhere would be good for both of them. This was also about efficiency. Not just for our limited fossil fuels, but emotionally. Why not have an uncomfortable, emotional introduction when you have three quarters of an hour to spend in a car together before a life event that will already be uncomfortable and emotional for all of us? Mae Mae and Matthew did not instantly bond during that one car ride. They talked about what they had in common: me and Ralph. There were some prolonged silences, Matthew told me on our own drive home from the wedding, but overall it was . . . nice. It was February in Minnesota, so the wedding should have been accessorized with a blizzard, or at least some sweeping, subzero winds. Instead, it was uncommonly warm that day. Not "Minnesota warm," which is anything above freezing, but warm-warm. Low seventies warm. This happens sometimes—a summer day plopped into the middle of winter—and it confuses not just the poor humans who had planned on a winter wedding and are now sweating in their February best, but confuses nature, too. Some trees were budding new leaves, a few perennials poked up through the still-too-frozen ground. Everything around us seemed stuck between two seasons, not quite sure if it was time to grow. I had been at the wedding venue for hours by the time Matthew and Mae Mae arrived. And the air that came with them through the door smelled almost like spring. They walked in step with one another: Mae Mae holding Ralph, and Matthew holding Ralph's bag of snacks and toys and other things he can't live without. They were still strangers to each other, but they were my family, and they'd grow to be each other's family, too.

Chapter Seventeen

In the Darkness

Uncle Dennis, my father's older brother, is special for many reasons, chief among them being that he has never used the internet.

Uncle Denny doesn't have an email address, because email doesn't work with typewriters. Since childhood, he's sent me letters typed on a typewriter or written in his perfect cursive, letters I keep to this day.

There is really no way around sorrow of this depth, this breadth. He writes after Aaron and my dad have died.

It simply has to be gone through. When I come to in the morning, before I'm fully awake, I have this vague, weighty sense of unease, as if there is something radically wrong with the world, and I don't quite know what it is.

Then I remember.

We continue to grope about in the darkness.

They are in the light.

That is what I've felt like all of these months, like I am groping about in the darkness, waking up in a world I hadn't expected to occupy. But there is no way through it except through it.

"Have you grieved?" my therapist asked, and I answered her quickly and with not a little annoyance.

"Yes." Next question?

Her next question was "How?"

"Uh, crying?"

She pushed, and I pushed back. In between checking things off my to-do list, achieving things, constantly staying in motion so as not to feel *too* much, I had cried sometimes!

Was that . . . not grief?

Sure. Yes. That is grief. But grief is so much more! Grief deserves a rebrand. Something like, Grief: so much more than just crying!

I was now seeing my therapist once a week, because something troubling was happening. Something deeply disturbing. I was, at times, *happy*. And that happiness triggered a deep, dark sadness to well up inside of me. I wanted it to stop, please.

I believed that these were two opposing forces at work, but they were just one: love. Grief is a by-product of love. We don't grieve what we don't love. We may feel slightly bummed about losing something we liked, but we don't *grieve* for it. And I had really, really loved.

That spark I felt with Matthew ignited something inside of me again. Not only the flames of new love, but my love for Aaron. Both of them were burning, and I felt like I would be consumed by it all. The grief that I had tried to skate through was catching up with me. And it was complicated. It was complicated because there was just so much of it! Aaron had been sick our entire marriage. I'd lost our second child at twelve weeks. My dad had died. And the world had just kept turning. Had my father died and my husband been healthy, I'd have leaned on Aaron. Had Aaron died and my dad been healthy, I'd have leaned on my father and my entire family. When both happened, I did expect everyone to rally around me, to hold me up by the armpits and launch me back into the world. But being Midwestern, I kept those expectations to myself, and quietly tallied how often they were not met. That huge wave of love and attention and help we received in the midst of Aaron's death had slowly evaporated. Not maliciously, but because people can't spend their entire lives focused on meeting your needs when they have their own lives to attend to. Why did my siblings—my best friends— not understand that I needed them to abandon their own lives and families and focus all of their attention on me? Why did they not show up, without being asked, to help me parent my child? To help me hang my Christmas lights or rake my leaves? Why didn't I ask them to? My self-isolation reinforced my belief that I was alone in this, that nobody could possibly understand. Nobody could possibly stand to be with all of this pain.

Except that Matthew totally could. Cue grief explosion.

One night, I sat up reading as Matthew slept. Under the covers, I noticed his legs, strong and healthy. And then they weren't his legs anymore, and it wasn't my bed. I was back in the hospital bed with Aaron, his thin legs—just bone covered in pale skin—sinking into the mattress. When I came back, I was crying, and Matthew was awake.

"What's the matter? What happened?"

I pushed him away and took my phone to the guest room, where I called Moe. It was after midnight, and she answered immediately.

It took minutes for me to say anything, and she waited.

"I get it." She said, "Aaron's dead. And Matthew's not."

That's exactly it. Aaron's dead. And Matthew isn't. The two facts are not related to one another, but they push against one another in my brain and in my heart. Because I get Matthew, and Matthew gets me, and Aaron just . . . died. That's objectively unfair.

"What *would* be fair?" my therapist wants to know. I don't have an answer. That we all die, but just a little bit? That we all end up alone, and lonely, forever?

Once, when a near-stranger was admiring the ring on my right finger, I explained to her that it had been a gift from Aaron. "Oh," she said, then gestured toward Matthew. "How does *he* feel about that?" The implication was that it must bother Matthew greatly, me parading this simple piece of brass around, a physical reminder that I loved another human.

"Well," I wanted to say, "as you can imagine, just the *sight* of it throws him into a jealous rage. He wants to wipe Aaron and his memory from the face of this earth and from my brain and my heart! I'm surprised he hasn't chopped off my finger yet!"

But I can't say that, because it isn't true. Aaron is not a four-letter word in our world. He's there in portraits that hang on our walls, in the tattoos on my body, in the child we had together who looks 110 percent like Aaron and 0 percent like me. But Matthew doesn't resent Aaron, or resent me for still loving him.

Of course people are shocked that Matthew can handle the fact that I love another man while I also love him. We're used to people having loved before, we aren't used to the idea that those loves could coexist, that they could happen at the same time. We assume that love is easily controlled and redirected, a series of switches you turn off and on, like the fuse box in your basement. I would personally love an emotional fuse box that let me feel one thing at a time, and if there are any scientists reading this, *please get on it*. I would love to feel just happy at happy times, and sad only at sad times. I would love to have clear delineations between my feelings. But as it is, they are all strands in a thread, all tangled up with one another.

I fell in love with Matthew, in spite of myself. Every attempt I'd made to scare him away had failed. He was sticking by me, even though I read him sad poetry, words that made me cry so hard I could barely even talk. And now I was snapping into flashbacks and crying openly because I was *safe*. Because I was in love. I had someone to hold me while I cried, and to take out the garbage for me. I had someone who could love me while I loved someone else. I wasn't alone in the darkness anymore. I was starting to see a light. And still I cried. And still, he loved me back.

Chapter Eighteen

Oops

never take naps. Even as a preschooler, I would lay (lie?) . . . I would *be* on my cot, belly up, staring at the ceiling while all the children around me snored softly. In college, when all my friends took pre-party snoozes, I'd sit on the couch watching *Laguna Beach* reruns and waiting for everyone to wake up so we could test out our fake IDs at Don Pablo's. Even when I had my first child, and everyone kept insisting that I sleep when the baby sleeps, I spent my maternity leave using his naps as a time to unload the dishwasher, catch up on my trashy magazines, or just exist without a small person touching me.

So when I woke up in a puddle of drool on my couch on a weekday, I was concerned. What the hell had happened and where did the past two hours go? My laptop was asleep on my chest, indicating that I had been in the middle of a work project. I'd started this project mid-morning. The clock claimed it was now afternoon. My body whispered "go back to sleep," and that is exactly what I did. When I woke again, it was time to pick up Ralph from daycare. My day was over. I'd gotten nothing done. And I still felt like I needed to sleep for another six hundred years.

For the next part of the story to seem rational, you should know that I have always turned to pregnancy tests in times of uncertainty. A sexual education that was based mostly in plant reproduction and the Virgin Mary (remember, Catholic school) meant that I have spent my life with an irrational fear of spontaneous impregnation. I took pregnancy tests before I was remotely sexually active, because who knows* how sperm is transmitted? Do we have proof that you can't get pregnant from sharing a toilet seat with a woman who had sex right before peeing and may have had a small amount of sperm on her body that was then transferred to the toilet seat, where it shimmied from the edge of your thigh right up into your vagina and up to a waiting egg?† Could this anomalous nap be indicative of a uterine interloper? Of course not. I'd been dating Matthew for just a few months, and I'd had maybe one period since my brutal miscarriage.

There was no possible way I could be pregnant, which is why I went to Walgreen's and bought a five pack of the name-brand tests and texted my daycare lady that I would be late picking up my toddler. It couldn't be in any way possible, which is why a hot-pink PREGNANT appeared immediately in the window as I was *still peeing on the stick*. Not remotely possible. But there it was. And standing in front of my tiny sink in my tiny bathroom, I watched my face react. I was shocked. I was happy! I was shocked that I was happy. And then I was sad.

Aaron and I had always agreed to have a big family. Or, more accurately, I wanted a big family and I knew I could wear him down

---

* Most people, including many children.
† Yes. This is not a thing.

until he agreed to want one, too. I came from a family of four kids, born over a spread of eleven years. Two girls, two boys. Our family dynamic was aggressive and loving and sometimes maddening. When my dad shouted "Hog pile!" it was a signal to us to leap onto one of our siblings, one on top of the other, to crush them with our love but also with our bodies. Our dinner table was loud. Our house was energetic and filled with physical altercations over the remote control.

That's the kind of household I imagined for Aaron and me: one where I would spend upwards of a decade shouting "this is why I can't have nice things!" while holding broken pieces of a lamp in front of dirty-faced kids who all blamed someone else for whatever had broken my favorite heirloom (or, more realistically, an impulse purchase from Target).

That window—if it was ever really open—slammed shut the moment I saw that blood.

Just two months before, we'd been laying in our bed, his hand on my stomach. He was dying, yes, but we didn't say it out loud. Instead, we focused on the small life that was blooming inside of me while his had begun fading. His smile—once electric, beaming—was a small upward pull that only the right side of his face could manage. I watched his beautiful hands, now whittled down into fingers slenderer than mine, gently sink into the flush of my swelling tummy.

I cried for a lot of reasons after I miscarried our second baby. One: I had miscarried a baby. Two: I had ruined the very end of Aaron's life. Three: Ralph would be an only child. That miscarriage had been the first in a Triple Crown of losses that happened so quickly one after the other I didn't even have *time* to be sad about the first one.

Aaron was meant to be a dad, and he loved being Ralph's papa. Aaron sang Bruce Springsteen as he rocked Ralph to sleep and coordinated his chemo naps with Ralph's nap schedule. The two of them were each other's favorite person, and I was happily the third wheel. Aaron's cancer seemed to be held at bay, and because I am a very pragmatic and logical person, I credited not the team of medical experts working with Aaron, but our child. As Ralph approached two years old, Aaron's cancer advanced. For the first time, he seemed truly *sick*. He couldn't drive a car. He slept around eighteen hours a day. He had gotten so weak he couldn't lift Ralph, who would instead climb into Aaron's lap and lay for hours, sucking his thumb. If Ralph had kept Aaron alive, then surely another baby would do the same thing. If Ralph was the living embodiment of Aaron's legacy, why *wouldn't* I have another? Why wouldn't I want Aaron to live on in as many people as I could possibly create inside of me? I had assumed that Aaron's cancer had given us an immunity to other kinds of tragedy. What kind of a God is going to let you miscarry when your husband has brain cancer?*

Over a year had passed since that miscarriage, since my dad's death, and then Aaron's. My brain had turned to goo. I couldn't remember if I'd turned off the burner after dinner, or where my car keys were. I couldn't remember the day or time of the meeting, or where I parked my car when it was time to leave because I had the details about both mixed up. I couldn't remember having my period, either, but that could be explained away like all of the other things I was missing. My brain and my body were busy surviving. Any extraneous activities would be ceased until there was more bandwidth. I vaguely remembered reading something in *Seventeen* magazine two decades ago that had instilled a lot of additional preg-

---

* God would like to point out that she's not in charge of every single thing that happens in our lives, and also she was focused on some other, big-picture things.

nancy anxiety in me during my teen years. Maybe you didn't *need* to have a period to get pregnant?

All of this is making it sound as if this were an unplanned pregnancy, which, of course it wasn't unplanned. Matthew and I had been dating for exactly four months before I took that test. Which puts the date of conception somewhere around the three-month mark. Which is . . . atypical? No, we did not say to one another "three months seems like the right mark to really solidify a blended family with the glue of a small baby." But we also didn't say "let's not get pregnant right now." We *did* spend a lot of time *talking* about a baby, and a lot of time engaged in activities that could have resulted in a baby. I will say this: if we are having sex and you ask if you need a condom and I say "don't worry about it," you should maybe worry about it.

There was no need to tell Matthew just yet. It was so new. Anything could happen. And the idea of breaking his heart like I'd broken Aaron's was too much. I'd wait. Just a few weeks, maybe more. Make sure this one was here to stick. *Then* I'd tell him. He'd be happy, right?

The baby I'd lost just before Aaron died would have been ten months old by now. That pregnancy had ended at eleven weeks and six days, *so* close to that magical twelve-week mark that even though I knew that pregnancy loss is common, and that there was nothing I could have done to change the outcome, it still felt like I'd jinxed it somehow. Maybe I'd told too many people, too soon? Maybe it was that jog I took? Or sleeping on my stomach?

There was no use telling Matthew just yet, not when there was still a chance that I could lose this. That anxiety was directly at odds with my excitement and wonder.

Some days, driving to pick up Ralph, I let myself imagine another car seat in the back of my station wagon, Matthew's daughter in between them, his son . . . wait, my car wasn't going to be big enough for all of us. Neither was Matthew's. Did we need a minivan? Those were my favorite days, the ones where I thought about the fact that only three kids could fit in the backseat, the days I let myself believe we were going to have four.

Chapter Nineteen

Sad Nora and the Secret Baby

REASONS I DON'T WANT THIS BABY:

- Matthew and I have been dating approximately five minutes and babies are more permanent than tattoos.
- Matthew and I don't even live together and I'm not moving to his side of town because I like where I live, and I like my life.
- Ian is fourteen and it will ruin his life.
- Sophie is ten and it will ruin *her* life.
- Ralph is three and it will ruin *his* life.
- I am thirty-four and it will ruin *my* life.
- Matthew is thirty-seven and it will ruin *his* life.
- I won't love this baby as much as I love Ralph.
- I won't love this baby at all.
- I won't love this baby, and the baby will know, and then reject me, and then I *really* won't love it.
- I won't love this baby and everyone will know and think I'm an awful person.

- This baby is somehow a sign that I didn't love Aaron enough.
- This baby is a sign that I don't know how birth control works.
- This baby deserves better than me (can I transfer this pregnancy to a worthy friend?).

REASONS I WANT THIS BABY:

I WANT THIS BABY.

It's not that I wasn't excited to be pregnant, it's just that I didn't want anyone to know about my pregnancy, and I didn't want to talk about it, and having a baby grow inside of me felt like a betrayal to my dead husband, our dead baby, and our love in general. In other words, things were *fiiiiiiine* and everything was great.

Things *were* fine and everything *was* great: I was in a beautiful relationship with a man who loved me. Our baby was growing inside of me, strong and healthy. My boobs had grown into absolutely perfect C cups. I cannot stress that last point enough: my boobs were absolute perfection. They looked like they'd been molded by the world's most talented plastic surgeon. The kind of boobs where you think "Did she?" then, noticing how absurdly perfect and natural they looked, are forced to correct yourself. "Of course, she didn't. Nobody's fake boobs could look *that* good." I spent a lot of time admiring and documenting these boobs, for any future surgical needs. I did not spend the same amount of time admiring or documenting the belly beneath them.

All my pregnancies have been unlikely. We had just a few vials of Aaron's pre-radiation, pre-chemo sperm, and the success rate of IUI with the added fertility drugs was quoted to us as anywhere around nine to sixteen percent. I'm not a gambler or a statistician or even someone who took real math classes in college, but I am a person who believes in the power of feelings, and those numbers *felt* very low to me. After the insemination, we had the infamous two-week wait: fourteen days spent with an uncanny focus on my uterus. That twinge I just felt—was it a fertilized egg implanting into the wall of my uterus? Or did I eat too much for lunch? My mind operated with an acute awareness of everything that could be potentially happening inside my body, which meant that for two weeks, I was only *pretending* to be at work, clicking all over a PowerPoint or a spreadsheet, while imagining the potential explosion of cells happening inside of me. The blood test itself was fast—the phlebotomist does not make small talk while she fills small vials with your blood—and then, it was back to work, back to waiting. My brain then shifted its focus from my insides to my phone. Everything felt like the buzz of my ringer, even when I banished my phone to my purse, under my desk. When the phone did ring, it was a nurse who knew I was currently creating a human being inside of me. I left work immediately after that phone call, because who can possibly work while they are growing a human life?* That secret glowed inside of me, so brightly it felt as if anyone who looked at me would see it: a golden orb beaming magic from the inside. Aaron and I danced in our living room when I told him he would be a father. We wiped tears from each other's faces. It felt like a miracle. It felt like possibility. It felt like everything I had ever rolled my eyes at in my life was now located in my lower abdomen.

This pregnancy felt different from the one that had given us Ralph, and the one that we lost. That happiness I felt when I took the test was at odds with this darker feeling that was taking over. As the pregnancy progressed, it felt like I was growing a black cloud inside of me, a sadness that coordinated with the size of the baby

---

* Women throughout the history of the world raise their hands.

itself. Today, your sadness is the size of a sesame seed. Today, your sadness is the size of an orange.

Our children, at this point, are spread across eleven years. We've spent the last few months marveling at how easily this group of five has melted into a family. How the Bigs started calling Ralph their little brother, without us ever even suggesting it. How the Bigs asked to spend the night at The Dollhouse, or to tag along to Ralph's soccer games even though he only ever just stands there, in the middle of the gym, absolutely refusing to participate. We'd reached an accidental equilibrium that none of us ever expected. Sophie invited me to orchestra concerts, Ian walked off the soccer field and scooped Ralphie up in his arms. Matthew and I *shared Google calendars.* We'd become a family.

As solid and average as our family felt, it also felt rare and fragile. We were all still new to one another. The Bigs spent some of their time at another house, with another parent. They had a whole different life that Matthew had separated from, that Ralph and I were not a part of. I knew from experience that a baby could make everything better. Or worse.

I was two years old when my parents brought my little brother Patrick home from the hospital. He is now a beloved member of my family, but at the time? He was just a pile of screaming flesh, always red with anger. He screamed constantly, and I remember looking at him and wondering "Why did my parents do this to us?" Patrick grew into a toddler who refused to look at the camera for family photos, a child who could not possibly do his homework on time, and a teenager who graduated our high school as an act of mercy by the school president, who knew he was the last McInerny he'd ever have to see. Patrick was a pain in the butt right up through his early twenties, when he fell in love and fixed himself and is now consistently in the top two of our mother's Favorite Child Ranking System, which she keeps on her fridge and is only partially a joke. Even good babies are a lot of work. They are completely helpless. They cry. They take up a lot of time and attention. That's attention that many new couples spend on one another, not on sleepless nights and dirty diapers and warming bottles and pumping milk. That's attention that the other kids deserved and needed. Ralph and Ian and Sophie had each had their worlds fall apart already, and I wanted this new world we had made to feel as safe and solid as possible. A baby did not feel safe. A baby did not feel solid. Babies don't just cry. They sometimes die. My last baby had died. Babies die all the time, sometimes before they're born and sometimes while they're born and sometimes after! What if this one died? What if this one died, and we broke all the kids' hearts, and our family fell apart? My concern, though, wasn't just for the kids. My concern was for me. Maybe my concern was primarily for me, but considering the kids first made me feel like a slightly better person for all of the ambivalence I felt toward this pregnancy. I had just finally gotten my life onto solid ground. My first book—about my dead husband—was about to be published. Did I really want to stand up in front of a bunch of strangers to talk about Aaron with a belly full of another man's baby? Could I survive another miscarriage?

Ambivalence led to shame. Inside me, a human being was knitting itself together from the McDonald's French fries and Coca-Cola I was consuming every single day. All around me, I had dear friends whose hearts were breaking because having a baby turned out to be harder than we thought it would be when we were in our twenties, popping a birth control pill at the bar and washing it down with cheap beer. I'd wanted siblings for Ralph, and here they were: all three of them. I'd wanted more life, more love, and here it was. What in the actual hell was wrong with me? And what was going to snap me out of this? All of this drama was mine alone. Matthew didn't know yet. To him, I was just a sleepy girlfriend with great boobs who cried a lot. How would I tell him, this man who had first heard "I'm pregnant" at twenty-two, and had wept in grief and shame at the news, so sure his life as he knew it was completely over? I wasn't afraid that Matthew would weep, that he would be upset. I wasn't afraid of his reaction at all, really. Matthew in his late thirties is just too steady to be rocked by something as little as a zygote.

Pinterest and Instagram and YouTube would have you believe that the only way to tell your partner that you're pregnant is through presenting them with a complicated riddle, ordering a hand-painted sign from Etsy, or painting "baby on board" across your naked stomach and standing around until your partner notices you've somehow painted legibly on your own torso. I kid you not, these are all suggestions I found while Googling "How do I tell my boyfriend I am pregnant?" I suppose I could have just *said* it, with my mouth and my words, but social media had poisoned my brain into believing that words were not enough! I had to have a thing, a theme, something to *hand* him.

I settled for a pacifier, one of Ralph's old cast-offs, which I had found in a junk drawer. I dusted it off and put it in a small box, which I handed to Matthew one evening when he came over. We were seated in our usual spot, making out like a couple of teenagers, when I paused. "Hey," I said, "I got you something," standing up to retrieve the box from my mantel.

"It's really just *part* of a gift. You'll get the rest in a few months."

He smiled, like I was the most thoughtful person in the world, getting him a complicated two-stage gift. I watched him expectantly while he opened the box and pulled out the pacifier.

What did his face say? Was he happy? Excited? Terrified?

He was, actually, *completely confused.*

"So . . . what?" he asked, looking at me with an empty expression, the kind you make when someone has just told you they found you *the perfect gift*, the one that is *so you* and you open it and realize, *this person does not know me at all*. It's the kind of expression where your body forces your face to go blank, because your body knows that your brain is thinking "What the actual *fuck*?"

"What's the other part?" he asked, as if just asking "what?" wasn't a clear enough question.

"I'm . . . pregnant?" I asked him, smiling like a hostage.

The pieces clicked together in his brain. This was a baby pacifier. The second part of the gift was a baby, who would use that pacifier when it arrived in a few months. His face rearranged itself into something resembling disbelief.

"I thought you couldn't get pregnant," he said softly, not with anger, but with wonder.

"Me too," I laughed. He smiled with his whole face, his hand rushing to my stomach, his mouth finding my own. That little storm cloud inside of me lightened up. We were happy.

My spirituality is something my father would not approve of. Primarily because even the word *spirituality* irked him. To Steve, you were either religious or you weren't. To him, "spirituality" was a nothing word used by people with no solid beliefs. It's the Diet Coke of theology: calorie free and probably a carcinogen. But I don't know what else to call my little pastiche of hunches, beliefs, and feelings. God: yes, although God is not an old man in the sky. Saints? Maybe. Jesus? A cool guy, but most of his followers are the worst. I also believe that there are many paths to whatever the summit is, that there is something other than just the world we live in. I still wasn't about to go to *church* but I did feel . . . spiritual? I don't know what else to call it when you're sitting next to a woman at a pop-up gift market, a woman with icy blue eyes that seem to stare into your soul, and she asks you if you'd like a reading, and all of a sudden she's lighting Palo Santo and holding your hand and the din of hundreds of women on the hunt for the perfect locally made craft melts away and it's just the two of you, holding hands, floating on a cloud. The stranger's name is Rachel, and that ethereal feeling remains with me long after our few minutes together are over. I know that my dad would think of this all as total bullshit, but Rachel isn't a psychic. She is an intuitive healer; it says so right on her business card. I remember everything she says and replay it in my head over and over and over.

She was quiet for a long time before she spoke. She says that I am emanating fear. I am afraid to fail. This is because I am a *creator*, and creating means offering up your gifts to the world. I am afraid that my two biggest creations to date are at odds with one another, that they could easily cannibalize each other, or invalidate each other. My face is hot, and my eyes are burning, and she continues. They are not at odds with one another, she tells me, but my creations both have their own purpose and destiny. They are two sparks that will help my own fire burn brighter. One is meant as a light for the world. The other is meant as a light for my family. My work is done. I just need to let them shine.

Chapter Twenty

Memorial Day

I gave Matthew the job of telling The Bigs about the baby. He took them out for dinner at a terrible restaurant they love, a cavernous space in a far-off suburb that bills itself as a Japanese steakhouse, and specializes in pouring teriyaki sauce on everything. Because the kids were allowed to pick the restaurant, and because of Matthew's generally awkward demeanor, Ian and Sophie assumed that their dad wanted to announce the news of his terminal illness. Maybe that's why they cheered when they learned there would be a new sibling arriving in November.

Ralph and I had had our own little meeting that same night, but I didn't need to announce anything to Ralph. Just weeks after I took that pregnancy test, Ralph and I flew to New York City for a few days. In the cab from LaGuardia, he snuggled into me and gazed out the window, sucking his thumb.

"Mama," he asked, "are you pregnant?"

The cabdriver's eyes immediately darted to the rearview mirror, and locked with mine.

"What?" I asked trying to hide my panic behind a hearing issue.

"Are. You. Pregnant." Ralph reiterated, less like a three-year-old toddler and more like Maury Povich trying to interrogate a particularly belligerent guest.

I said, "Yes," and he nodded. But I had a follow-up.

"Ralphie," I said, "do you know what pregnant means?"

"You're pregnant."

Okay then. I do believe that children are highly intuitive and know way more than we think they do. That part of me, yeah, kind of believes that maybe Aaron put the idea in his head. I also believe that they are constantly absorbing information from the world around them, and it's more likely he heard that word at daycare or at the checkout line at Target than he did from me. Ralph never really asked about me being pregnant again, but the day Matthew told the Bigs, I gave Ralphie a book about a baby growing in a mom's belly, and he rolled his eyes. "Can I have another present?" he asked.

The Bigs wanted to talk about baby names, and where the baby would sleep. Each made a case for putting the crib in their room—they'd *happily* wake up in the middle of the night to snuggle their little sibling so Matthew and I could sleep. They'd only wake us up in case of a dirty diaper.

Crisis had been avoided. Our family would not be broken. This baby *would* be a light for our family.

We told the kids over Memorial Day weekend, when we'd have three days to hang out together. It was beautiful weather. Minnesota decided to really have a spring, and our backyard was gorgeous and blooming. We set up our hammock and tilled the garden and made plans for our summer.

I was the first to wake up on Monday morning, and I snuck out the front door and into the car. The co-op is just a few blocks away, with doughnuts and good coffee. It was already warm out, a whisper of the coming summer in the air. I felt so smug. At home, three beautiful children and a handsome man were still sleeping in my sweet little house. I was at a co-op buying organic coffee and gluten-free doughnuts. I had plans to go to the nursery and buy flowers for my window boxes. Outside, my station wagon was parked in the very best spot in the parking lot. Inside, a little baby was growing who everyone was excited to meet. That little baby was also busy rearranging my organs, and I really, really needed to pee.

There was blood when I wiped. A lot of blood. There was blood in the toilet bowl and soaked into my underwear. The light was going out. At a fucking organic food co-op.

I shoved a handful of toilet paper into my panties and pulled up my jeans shorts and ran from the bathroom to the parking lot, drawing absolutely no attention to myself.

I'd done it again. I'd lost a baby. And now I would break Matthew's heart and Ian's heart and Sophie's heart and Ralphie's heart the way I'd broken Aaron's. I had been so arrogant and stupid. So careless. I had gone to the midwife, but I hadn't taken my vitamins regularly. I had told my family, and Matthew's, but hardly any of my friends. I'd been ambivalent about this baby, and it had known. It had known it wasn't truly wanted and had decided to cut its losses.

Matthew and the kids were snuggled on the couch reading the newspaper and watching cartoons. I snuck from the back door up to my bedroom and texted Matthew. Yes, a text. I texted the father of my dead baby to let him know what was going on.

I'm losing the baby. Stay downstairs with the kids and act natural.

Clearly, I am an expert in interpersonal communication.

I knew I had to go to the hospital, and so I called Moe. Moe was why Matthew and I met, and she had been thrilled by the news of this pregnancy. As someone who was done having babies, Moe considered this pregnancy to be spiritually hers, as well. "How's our baby?" she'd text me, and I'd let her know what the app said was going on in my uterus. Moe was in the car before I could even get the full sentence out, barreling across town to get me. And then I called the nurse line. The first time I'd called, a year and a half before, they'd assured me that nothing was wrong. A little blood was no big deal. But this time was a lot of blood. "Oh, honey," the nurse whispered to me, "you need to go in. I'm so sorry." I thanked her for her service to the women of the world, and I laid back down in bed. Matthew had texted me back.

Can I please come up?

My body said yes, please, come up here and lay with me. Put your warm, tan hands on my belly and make this stop. Make this not be happening. My brain told my thumbs to say something else.

No. Stay with the kids. Don't freak them out.

I don't know what my long-term plan was. I would have to see Matthew and the kids eventually. But until then, until I got to the hospital and knew *for sure* that the baby was gone, I could stay in this suspended version of reality, the one where morning light was streaming through our bedroom windows, where I could hear Matthew and the kids splitting doughnuts downstairs in the dining room. I heard Moe's car bounce up our driveway. The slam of our front door, and her clogs clomping up the stairs.

I love you.

I'm sorry.

It was the same emergency room I'd been in the day that Aaron had been diagnosed with a brain tumor. The same one we'd come to on the day he'd entered hospice. I'd been there as his person, his caregiver. And now, I was here as the patient. I was the one in a backless gown, laying in a bed and waiting. I was the one who knew that something was desperately wrong inside of me, waiting for help. The emergency room was short-staffed because of the holiday weekend. It was a lot of blood, that's for sure, they all agreed. They'd need to get an ultrasound of my belly, but they needed to find someone who could work the machine. An ultrasound would confirm my baby was dead. And then, I could decide what to do. But I already knew what I was going to do. I was going to cry and break things. I was going to hate myself for the rest of my life, because I had killed this baby with my own emotional confusion. I was going to have to tell Matthew and his stupidly beautiful blue eyes that the baby was gone because I hadn't cared enough about it. I was also going to have my body to myself and go on a book tour without worrying about what anyone would think of me. I was going to get what I'd dreaded, and what I deserved. I was going to be broken, all over again. How do you mourn a baby you weren't always sure you wanted, and hadn't really told anyone about? I called my mom and choked my way through telling her that she had to tell my siblings.

It took six hours for an ultrasound tech to make her way into the hospital. They pushed my bed along the same hallways that Aaron had been pushed through. The ultrasound tech was quiet as she warmed up the goo and spread it gently across my stomach. I was twenty weeks along, and barely showing. I'd been proud of that with Ralph—how at six feet tall I could be nine months pregnant and look like a college freshman who had just discovered the soft serve machine in the cafeteria. "Oh," the tech said, "your baby is right here."

I rolled my eyes toward the monitor, waiting to see that familiar digital ghost, frozen on screen.

My baby was there. And alive. Wiggling, waving, kicking. Alive.

Moe screamed. I screamed. The tech screamed.

"Call Matthew!" I shouted, and Moe stepped into the hall.

"Our baby is alive!" Moe shouted, and the tech squeezed my hand.

"Say hello, Mama!" the tech whispered to my belly, and my baby kicked its little frog legs, completely oblivious to the many hearts that had almost broken that day.

"Hello, Baby," I whispered.

Matthew and the kids were in the backyard when we arrived, and I snuck back upstairs and into bed, still unsure of what to say to any of them. The doctor who discharged me had basically told me it was "just one of those things." But I was fine. The baby was fine. Moe headed to the yard to hang out with the kids, and I heard Matthew bang in through the back door and run up the stairs until he was next to me, mouth on my neck, warm hand on my belly, tears soaking into my hair.

We didn't say anything. We just lay there, quietly, happy in the way you can only be when you've been on the edge of devastation, crying for all the ways your hearts could have broken, but haven't. Not yet.

I'LL BE BETTER

I swore I would be different. While I was laying in that hospital bed I had promised God, The Universe, Yoda, and every other force that could possibly give a crap about my uterus that I would love and cherish this baby. That I would celebrate this pregnancy the way it deserved to be celebrated.

I started taking a multivitamin *every day* and going back to barre classes to strengthen something called my pelvic floor. I bought a few small onesies and made a list of baby names. And that's basically it.

There was no ecstatic Instagram announcement, or baby shower. And I didn't really tell anyone I hadn't told before. Outside of a few friends and family, I just sort of wore a lot of shapeless clothes and pretended to the rest of the world that nothing was happening inside my body.

Around this same time, I saw an article about the writer Chimamanda Ngozi Adichie, who had recently had a baby without making any sort of formal announcement. She was quoted as saying, "I just feel like we are living in an age when women are supposed to perform pregnancy," and I felt instantly recognized. I didn't want to perform pregnancy. I didn't want to make a chalkboard sign or line up some sneakers for a photo shoot. I didn't want to pose with the ultrasound over my belly, a look of false shock on my face.

Because performing this pregnancy would mean performing everything that came along with this pregnancy. It would mean showing people the depression and anxiety that grew along with this baby. Every twinge in my belly felt like an indication that things were going wrong. Did I feel the baby kick today? Why couldn't I remember? A baby is supposed to make you happy. And I was happy. But I was also terrified and devastated. The happiness I felt didn't replace my sadness, it just sort of mixed in with it. Everything good in my life had a sad aftertaste. Everything good in my life had come from loss. Everything sweet was just a little bitter.

If you're thinking, "Hey, didn't you mention depression earlier in this book? And therapy? What happened with that?"

What happened with that was that I went off my antidepressant, cold turkey, when I found out I was pregnant and didn't bother to consult a medical professional beyond Google.com. That was . . . a bad idea.

It was also a bad idea to become overwhelmed with my schedule and decide that the fat that could be trimmed was therapy.

I told myself that I wasn't performing my pregnancy, that I was keeping it close to me, and to my family, because it was just for us. I was telling the truth, but only part of it. Because the whole truth was that I was in the thick of antepartum depression, which is a medical way of saying that I was pregnant and depressed as heck. This pregnancy would overlap with the anniversary of my pregnancy loss, and the due date was just a week before Aaron's deathaversary. How could I spend that day in remembrance of Aaron when I'd have a fresh human attached to me? The baby's due date was right alongside another due date: I had pitched and sold a podcast idea to American Public Media, and its planned launch date was the same week I was supposed to be having a baby.

Terrible, Thanks for Asking was going to be a narrative podcast where I interviewed people about the way it really feels to go through life's hardest moments. Preparing for that first season, I spoke to a woman who had still-birthed her full-term son, Henry; a man whose grandparents' murderer was being released from prison; a rape survivor; a woman with a traumatic brain injury and severe memory loss . . . you get the picture. The podcast isn't (all) depressing, but immersing myself in these stories while trying to manage my own complicated feelings was harder than I could admit to myself. But I couldn't slow down, or push the launch date back. I couldn't even admit to my colleagues that I was pregnant. Okay, I could have. But I didn't. Because slowing down would have meant truly sitting in all of these heavy, uncomfortable feelings, and because the world is still a sexist place, and I didn't trust that the show would have the same support behind it if people knew that I was going to need time off to take care of a baby in just a few months.

I had chosen the name of the podcast because it was the exact opposite of what I'd told people after Aaron died. "How are you?" is not just a question we lob at one another as small talk, it's a question that is asked more pointedly when your life is in turmoil. People asked me how I was, and I assured everyone around me that I was totally fine, that everything was as good as could be expected. I measured my worth by how much I could bear, and how much of it I could bear on my own. "Fine" by "fine" I had built myself a lonely little prison. I was desperate to be honest with people about how hard things were, but unable to say it aloud.

"Let's all be honest!" was the ethos of my show, while I continued to lie and tell everyone who asked me how I was that I was "fine!"

My midwife wasn't buying it. The baby's heartbeat was strong. Everything was looking great. And how was I feeling?

Uh, fine?

She nodded in the way that can only mean "bullshit" and said nothing. The silence sat until I filled it myself.

"I'm actually . . ."

It felt like I explained myself for hours, but it couldn't have taken more than five minutes. I was devastated by the sight of my son Ralph's spine poking through his pale skin in the bathtub. I wept just describing it, how tender and human he was, how someday he would get old and die and would he be lonely? Some days it felt like I was watching the world from inside glass, like one of those paperweights you can buy at T.J. Maxx that has a scorpion suspended in acrylic. I couldn't stop worrying about the baby—could she check its heart again?—I was afraid I wouldn't love it once it arrived. That I would never love the baby like I loved Ralph, or Aaron, or Matthew, or the other kids. Why did I feel like that? Why was I so awful?

She listened with tenderness, and soon we were joined by the OB/GYN and we were talking about what I could do.

I pinky-swore to go back to my therapist, and I pinky-swore I would pick up the prescription they wrote for me. What kind of mother needs a prescription to make her feel okay while she's performing the miracle of life? ALL KINDS OF MOTHERS! Tall ones, short ones, funny ones, mean ones. All kinds of moms need help during their pregnancy because building a life inside of you is not always fun, and neither are baby shower games where you melt candy bars inside diapers and try to guess what the baby pooped out! Most of pregnancy is your organs being rearranged and your hormones going haywire and your boobs hurting and being annoyed when your partner breathes. Would my baby be okay with me popping some SSRIs while it finished roasting inside of me? Well, it sure as hell wouldn't be doing well if mommy had a total mental breakdown, would it?

That night, I tapped two small white pills into the palm of my hand and washed them down with ice water. Matthew played with my hair until I fell asleep, hand over my belly.

I was not great. I was not fine. But I would be better.

Chapter Twenty-One

Armless

I am an intense sleeper. I either cannot fall asleep at all or I fall so deeply asleep that waking up feels like I am being plucked from the deepest realm of consciousness like one of those claw games that nobody ever wins at the bowling alley. When I sleep, I sleep so hard that I wake up sore: stiff neck, locked-up jaw, brain filled with whatever hallucinations my subconscious decided to serve me. I keep paper and pens by my bed to write down any late-night ideas I have in case they are so brilliant they must be remembered, and so I can write down dreams that seem important, for later analysis. The reality of this practice is that I have dozens of Post-it notes that say things like "the hummus story" or "I am missing both my arms."

That second one, though, means something to me. After Aaron died, I dreamed I was walking through the world completely armless. The people in my dream life fell into two camps: those who pretended not to notice my armlessness, and those who were irritated by what they felt was my obsession with it. "NORA!" I recall one of them dream shouting at me at the dinner table when I cried that I couldn't eat the soup on account of having no arms. "Use your FEET!"

I spent a year drinking soup with my feet. Not literally, but I'm trying to unpack the psychological obviousness of this dream and draw some parallels here, okay?

The hard part about having a not-super-planned pregnancy while you're a parent dating another parent whose children each have established lives on opposite sides of a decently sized metro area is . . . everything. Where do you live? Who uproots whom?

Matthew and I didn't want to rush anything, but the gestation of a human child tends to follow a pretty standard timeline, which meant the baby would arrive about a year after Matthew and I had met. That's a pretty okay amount of time to decide to move in together, but it wasn't just *us* moving in together. Ralph was three, so his entire world was me and whatever I said it was. Matthew's kids were older. They had schools and friends and an entire life that revolved around a five-mile radius in a northern suburb. Matthew's house was too small to fit all of us. My house was the perfect size, but on the wrong side of town. *Everything* about my life—my family, The Dollhouse, Ralph's daycare—was on the south side. It may be a matter of a few miles, but the geography of our lives has real meaning. I was used to my grocery store, my side of the freeway, being within walking distance of my family.

There were a few options:

1. Ralph and I move to Matthew's side of town.

2. Matthew and his kids move into The Dollhouse.

3. We find a new home, move in together, and compromise.

4. My proposal: everything stays the same.

Why should the arrival of a very small person force us into a huge move? The baby could stay with Ralph and me and would see Matthew and The Bigs regularly. No big moves, just an extra little person joining the little club we were forming.

This rankled my mother more than a little bit.

"Well," she huffed at me one day, "it sounds like you don't even *need* him."

I nodded in enthusiastic agreement.

"Exactly!" I said, ignoring her obvious irritation.

I didn't need Matthew, and I was proud of that. Moreover, I didn't want to lose that. I'd grown attached to my own armlessness, and my ability to drink soup with my feet. I had found out how strong I was, and I didn't want to lose that, either.

Living with Matthew—*marrying* Matthew? That was too traditional for the New Nora. I wanted to stay independent, a marvel of modern single-motherhood.

Weirdly, Matthew didn't love the idea of being a part-time father to his unborn child, or the idea of maintaining two separate residences.

And neither did the kids. We'd decided to let them take the lead on how much time we spent together. I didn't want to be a person who just showed up in their lives one day and dominated their Dad Time, so Matthew and I decided that we'd only hang out if his kids specifically requested it. And they requested it all the time. They were the ones who asked if they could sleep over at The Dollhouse and claimed "their rooms." They were the ones who asked when we would all live together. They were the reason why I let Matthew be my arms.

I still don't need Matthew. Yes, he makes my coffee and folds my underwear and knows the kids' schedules by heart and remembers literally everything about our lives. My life would devolve into chaos without him, but I still don't need him. I can do all of this on my own. But I don't have to. I don't need him, but I choose him. Happily.

STORMTROOPERLUCKYCHARM

I'll be honest, I wanted a girl. No, I insisted on a girl. I sent that fetus some heavy femme vibes, and came up with a flawless list of girl's names before Matthew told me some shocking news: I had no control over what kind of a baby was forming inside of me. The sex of this baby was determined by whatever sperm had reached the egg. This all came down to Matthew!

"This better be a girl!" I'd tease, waving a fist in his face, because yes, of course the goal is a happy and healthy baby, but is it so much to ask to have a happy and healthy baby that also opens you up to a whole new section of tiny clothes at Target? Ian wanted another little brother. Ralph wanted whatever Ian said he wanted. But Sophie was desperate for a sister. She spent her own money on a puffy pink dress she found on clearance at Target. It was a bit unseasonable for a baby whose expected arrival date was in mid-November, but she presented it to me as *the* outfit to bring the baby home in. I checked the tag: size twelve months, and told her we'd consider it. "Hello, sister!" she'd shout at my belly, and then look at her father pointedly.

"This better be a girl." Matthew would give us a nervous smile and cross his fingers.

We let the kids in on our baby name list, and listened to their suggestions. Sophie had suggested Scarlett and Elizabeth and Cress, all characters from books she was reading. Ralph had suggested StormtrooperLuckyCharm, based on his two main interests: Star Wars and sugary cereals. StormtrooperLuckyCharm did have a certain ring to it. It worked for any gender. It was unique. And so, until baby was born, that was its name. StormtrooperLuckyCharm.

Nearly four years had transpired between my first and second births, just enough time to wipe my memory completely clean. Ralph had arrived precisely on his due date, so I expected this baby would do the same. But two weeks before my due date, my water broke. That hadn't happened with Ralph, not in the movie-plot way it was now happening, with a telltale puddle on our kitchen floor. "Matty," I shouted, "grab the keys! StormtrooperLuckyCharm is coming!"

We kissed the kids good-bye, put our fifteen-year-old in charge of Sophie and Ralph, and headed to the hospital, holding hands. The hospital where I'd be delivering had built a shiny new birth center that looked more like a hotel than a hospital. Matthew dropped me off at the front, and I walked confidently to the front desk. "Hi," I said, smiling, "I'm having a baby."

The front desk attendant looked at me skeptically. Was I *sure*? I took it as a compliment. I was just so calm and collected, she couldn't believe I was in labor!

"Yes," I smiled, "my water broke!"

Twenty minutes later, we were walking back through the front door of our house without a baby.

"False alarm!" I told the kids. It wasn't a lie, it's just that the specific false alarm was that I had peed on the floor without realizing it.

StormtrooperLuckyCharm came one week later. This time, I waited until I was absolutely sure, until my legs were about to give way beneath me at the Blu Dot furniture outlet, before I told Matthew what I thought might possibly be happening. He fumbled for his car keys, but I told him we weren't leaving until we'd bought a coffee table and a bookcase.

Two hours later, we were back in the hospital/hotel and I was done having a baby.

"It's a . . . boy?" Matthew said timidly, offering up the slimy little worm creature I'd just birthed. The warm, wriggling little creature snuggled up on my chest. I was disappointed, okay? I was! I had one request, and I didn't get it. But it's hard to stay disappointed when a little tiny runt of a human opens his eyes for the first time and instantly recognizes you as the center of his world. It's impossible to stay disappointed when his oldest siblings burst into the hospital room and weep at the sight of him, marveling over his teensy tiny fingernails and his furry shoulders.

StormtrooperLuckyCharm got a real name, eventually. But it doesn't actually matter what it is, because everyone calls him Baby. There's a real chance he's going to grow up to be a full-grown adult male who answers to Baby, and I'm fine with that.

We'd naturally been worried about how the kids would or would not bond with Baby. There are fifteen years between Baby and his oldest brother, eight years between him and Sophie, nearly five between him and Ralph. And it hasn't mattered. Not a bit. Not a smidge. If anything, those age gaps play to his advantage. For Ralph, he is an easily manipulated playmate who will give up any toy if asked in a nice voice. For Sophie, he is basically a doll. And for Ian, he's . . . honestly? He's like his best friend. Baby's feet barely touched the ground the first year of his life. He needed only to glance at any object before Ian would offer it to him, or scoop him up in his arms to take the little prince to wherever he pointed.

For Baby's second Christmas, our family headed up to Duluth, Minnesota, for the Bentleyville Christmas Lights display. It's a few blocks' worth of giant, interactive Christmas lights that would make Clark Griswold jealous. It was well below freezing, but in Minnesota we believe that there is no bad weather, only bad clothing. Baby joined us for a below-zero stroll through the lights, pushed in his all-terrain stroller by his oldest brother.

We checked into the hotel ready to shake the chill from our bones, and discovered something truly astounding. Our room featured a giant tub. A giant tub in the middle of the living room. To an adult, this feature seems comical. To a child, it seems like the epitome of luxury and sophistication. Because we are Midwesterners, we of course packed our bathing suits on the off chance the hotel would have a pool. We hadn't anticipated that we'd have a tiny pool in the middle of our room. Who could imagine this kind of decadence?

Ian had turned on the TV, where, like it usually is on basic cable, the classic holiday film *The Devils Wears Prada* had just begun. "Leave it!" I shouted, and the saga of Andrea Sachs and Miranda Priestly unfolded while Baby attempted to stand on his own. I don't want to say that I missed our baby's first steps because I was busy watching a movie I'd seen about ninety-seven times before, but yeah, that is what happened. I missed his first shaky steps, but I looked over just in time to see him falter, and fall. It happened in slow motion, with his tender little head heading straight for the sharp edge of the open door. In equal slow motion, Ian dove across the room (okay, maybe a few feet), and caught Baby's noggin and body just in time. We all breathed a sigh of relief. Baby got back on his feet. Matthew filled the giant hot tub, and we all put on our swimsuits.

"You know what?" Ian said. "I don't know a lot of kids who can say that they spent their Christmas break in a bathtub with their entire family, watching *The Devil Wears Prada*, but I can't imagine anything better than this."

Me neither, dude. Me neither.

Chapter Twenty-Two

Should I Marry a Boy with a Brain Tumor?

I recently got a Facebook message from a twenty-two-year-old who was planning to marry her boyfriend, who she'd been dating for ages. I mean, she's twenty-two, so by *ages* I mean . . . since high school, probably. Her boyfriend has a brain tumor. Not a cancerous one, but one that can't be fully removed, one that could grow back at any time. And suddenly, the parents who were so excited to have a new son don't want their daughter hitching her wagon to a star that might burn out too soon. They assumed that the diagnosis meant that any wedding plans were off. Their twenty-two-year-old daughter certainly didn't intend to marry a man with brain cancer, did she? Well, uh, she did actually. Her parents weren't acting the part of movie villains, forbidding her to marry her beloved, but they didn't understand why she still planned to say "I do." It seemed crazy to them, which made it seem crazy to her.

I get a lot of messages asking me for advice. I have a clearly defined niche when it comes to relationship advice: people come to me when they need to know what to do when they find themselves at the intersection of Love and Disaster. The messages have a common theme: I am in love with a person. And this person now has something physically wrong with them. I still love them, but it's scary. What do I do?

"You married a man with a brain tumor," this girl wrote to me. "Do you regret it? Would you do it again? Am I CRAZY for still wanting to marry him? Help me."

The short answer is:

I did. Not for a moment. A million times, yes. You're not crazy. And, I can try.

The long answer is as follows. It sounds specific to brain cancer, but you can apply it liberally to any disaster you're facing.

I don't for a moment regret marrying Aaron. I wouldn't trade the four years we had together for any other healthy, still-alive man I could have married. I wouldn't trade them for anything except an impossible imaginary future where Aaron didn't get brain cancer and we got to grow old and squishy together and lived to be in our eighties and then died in our sleep, holding hands like a pair of otters.

I married Aaron just after his brain surgery to remove a tumor that turned out to be really, really bad brain cancer. We chose our wedding rings a few days before the ceremony. We let our moms choose the flowers and the colors of all the decor. But getting married—the actual legally binding part of it—wasn't really a choice.

I knew when I met Aaron that I had found the thing that they write books and songs about. I knew before his tumor was discovered that we would be married, and I knew the moment the doctor told us he had brain cancer that there was no way in hell I would be anywhere but by his side for whatever came next.

"Are you sure?" people very, very close to us asked. "This will get hard."

I was sure. I was sure on our first date, and I was sure the day we found his brain tumor. I was sure on the day we were married and the day that he died. I am sure now. The choices they were imagining I had were not choices at all. Yes, it was hard to watch the man I married get sick and sicker and die. It would have been hard even without those rings on our fingers.

Some people did see it as a choice between staying and going, as if my slinking away would have spared either of us any suffering. As if.

Others saw it as a choice between staying his girlfriend and getting married. In some ways, I get that. From the outside, watching someone marry a person with a terminal disease is probably like watching someone choose to step foot on the *Titanic* knowing its fate. But when it's your beloved, and your lives, it doesn't feel like you're choosing at all. It seems like you're taking the next natural step. Marriage is just a legally binding agreement that says you'll do life together. It also means, in the United States, that you have a right to help your beloved make life-and-death decisions. It means you have a right to be in the hospital room, to advocate for them. As a girlfriend or a boyfriend or a close friend that his family is really fond of . . . you just don't get the same considerations.

I can't tell you who to marry, or when to do it or not do it. And even though you're twenty-two and possibly still on their health insurance . . . NEITHER CAN YOUR PARENTS. Or your friends. Or your hair stylist (although of all the choices listed above, they are probably the best option you have for solid advice).

This is your life.

Yes, that is something you could read on a fake hand-painted sign you found at T.J. Maxx but dammit, sometimes those signs are on point, and that's why they're a decor staple in the Midwest.

This is *your* life, and the only certain thing about your life is that it will one day be over.

That's unfortunately true for all of us, even those without brain tumors, because science isn't a science and even if you never smoke a single cigarette, you can still get lung cancer. Even if you do yoga every day and never eat red meat, you can still have a heart attack. You can be a wonderful person and still get hit by a car. You're for sure gonna die and there's nothing you can do about that. Is that a scary thought that can keep us from living the lives we have? Sometimes. I personally don't want to be eaten by a bear or be bit by a rare spider and so I do not go camping. I am currently married to a man named Matthew, and you know what? He is going to die, too! And I have no idea when! I should probably text him right now and just make sure it hasn't happened yet! Is that scary? Yes. But the thing that is scarier than dying is living a life someone else picks for you.

So your parents don't think you should marry a guy with a brain tumor. Well, they're not marrying him. You are. And let me be clear, it will be like any of your friends' marriages: You will still watch Netflix and get irritated when he doesn't unload the dishwasher properly. You will disagree about money, about getting a dog, about whatever fits the bill of your particular partnership. His tumor won't change that, and neither will a ring on your finger. It will also be unlike any of your friends' marriages (unless you and I are friends). Your small disagreements will be just that: small disagreements. The Big Things in your marriage will be bigger than the worries of all your family and friends, all added up. Because you knew that when you promised " 'til death do we part" that death was coming before your retirement. You will watch an incurable disease eat him alive. You will live every vow you take, and it will be more sickness than health, and death will most certainly part you, probably sooner than later.

That is what you sign up for when you marry a man with a cancerous brain tumor.

Your boyfriend's brain tumor isn't cancerous, but still.

It is hard.

Life is, no matter what. Love is, no matter what. Even those friends of yours whose husbands and wives are currently strong and healthy whose lives are just *perfect* . . . will suffer. Even a perfectly curated Instagram feed cannot inoculate us from tragedy.

There is no choice we can make that will help us avoid heartache or suffering or loss, in some measure. Any person we love has a one hundred percent chance of dying, even the men parents think of as "safe choices" for their daughters.

I understand your parents' concerns because at twenty-two you are actually pretty much a zygote, all things considered. Twenty-two is so young! You are twenty-two chronologically, but situations such as ours have a way of aging us, of packing the wisdom of many more decades into us very quickly. You are certainly free to stay with your man and stand by him, as a girlfriend or as a friend. You are just as free to walk away, to find someone with no obvious health defects to build a life with. And you can hope nothing happens to either of you, but you just as certainly cannot guarantee it.

Your parents want to keep you from suffering, the same way they always have. When you were little, they placed special locks on the kitchen cabinets to protect your little fingers. They plugged up the electrical outlets to keep you from zapping yourself. They placed protective edges on the corners of the coffee table so you wouldn't crack your head open. That is why they are trying so hard to keep you from the great abyss of loss that might be ahead for you. But somehow, you still fell down. You still got bumps and bruises and maybe even stitches. And you kept going. Because as much as they'd like to, it isn't possible to bubble wrap a human from the dangers of the entire world.

You cannot bubble wrap and protect your heart from life, and why should you? It is meant to be used, and sometimes broken. Use it up, wear it out, leave nothing left undone or unsaid to the people you love. Let it get banged up and busted if it needs to.

That's what your heart is there for.

P.S. I am an ordained wedding officiant and am available most days because I don't have a social life.

Chapter Twenty-Three

Feeling Myself

f I'm ever famous enough to have my phone hacked, be prepared for a lot of partial nudes. Also, be prepared for many postpartum "does this look infected" full nudes. Basically, look at your own risk. Since Aaron died, I have been really into myself. I mean, really, really into myself. I have a hard time finding anything I don't like about my body. I like my big nose, and that my boobs are basically just nipples on a rib cage. I like my knock knees and my long feet. I like being taller than the average man.

I like myself so much that I have to document it. I have to have photographic evidence of how cute my butt is in the right underwear, and the way the light hits my collarbone when I'm waking up in the morning.

I like myself so much that it's a problem. This feeling is not socially acceptable. The socially acceptable rite of bonding among women is to share our self-criticisms, to relish in them. I've been a part of this sacred ritual for years. Put me in any living room in America with a group of women and a cheese tray, and in thirty seconds I'll know what every one of these strangers would change about their body. I'll assure them that their self-assessment is horribly inaccurate, that they have lustrous hair and ageless skin, that I'd gladly take their boobs if there were any such thing as a boob transplant. And then I'll offer up my own shortcomings to the group, so they can do the same for me. They'll tell me that my nose is enviable, and my acne is a figment of my imagination. Maybe for a second we'll be momentarily distracted by the cheese tray and can move on to deep debate about why we shouldn't be eating from it, followed by a list of the ways in which we are currently restricting our diets.

Sounds like a blast, right?

My friend Nicole is a talented photographer, and started to do boudoir shoots, which is a fancy way of saying "sexy photos of women in their underpants." Her photos are much better than the blurry photos I've taken in the mirror, which is why I found myself stripped down to my underwear, standing in front of Nicole and her camera in a sunny studio in Lowertown Saint Paul. Outside, it was cold and wintry. Inside, things were *hot*. Sorry, I can't help myself.

"You know," Nicole told me while I cupped my little boobs and pretended like something interesting was happening just outside the floor-to-ceiling windows, "you're the only woman who signed up to take these for herself." What she meant was that this sexy photo shoot wasn't a gift for a boyfriend or a girlfriend or a spouse or for luring in some internet dates. These photos were just for me.

"Have you done this before?" she asked, which yeah, is me bragging about what a good model I was. I said no, but I should have said yes, because I do this all the time. Not with a makeup artist and a light-soaked loft, but in my living room and bedroom and bathroom, with my phone and my mirrors.

Selfies have gotten a bad rap. We love to rip on them, and how vain and vapid it is to document one's own human existence.

But why? The urge to document ourselves and our lives is primal and old as dirt. Even your beautiful grandmother, the one who looked exactly like a pin-up? She'd have posted a billion selfies, too, if time and money and technology hadn't meant that her youth would be tragically relegated to a few black-and-white snapshots in a dusty shoebox somewhere.

Let's all stop pretending that selfies are an aberration of the high art we're creating with our smart phones or that posting a photo of yourself is somehow an interruption of the high-level discourse we are used to sharing on social media. You know what selfies can show you? Yourself. And you are worth looking at. You are worth marveling at.

Every day your body performs a series of complete and total miracles to keep you alive, and then your body does amazing things like creating another human, or running a mile, or getting to work on time, and to pretend like that isn't noteworthy is absurd. You are worth staring at in the mirror and capturing with whatever medium you have at your fingertips. You are worth paying a few hundred dollars to have someone else do it for you, if you can.

My body today is the same body that I used to hate, with the aftereffects of carrying and birthing two children. The thing that has changed, aside from the perpetual cycle of growing out and then cutting my bangs again, is my heart. Love changes us, and so does loss. There's something about having your husband die that really does a number on your confidence. Maybe it's just like getting an extra shot of YOLO, but after three years of watching the man I loved more than nachos and *Buffy the Vampire Slayer* combined die of a cancer that was hell-bent on destroying him, the many, many fricks I used to give about my body have disappeared, poof!

I would like to take the time here to acknowledge how many of you may have dislocated your eyeballs reading about how a blond white woman who has never been larger than a size ten has learned to accept a body that fits nicely and neatly into the white beauty standard. If it helps at all, I have always been ashamed of my body shame, which is . . . not healthy. But it should at least show you how absurd the whole notion is, that we were all sold and all bought the same lie, that the best thing our bodies could do was to conform, and be as good and as small as possible. The best thing that our bodies do is just *exist*. They show up and carry us through this world.

Aaron was sick for three years. I memorized the beat of his heart. I watched him be wheeled out of two brain surgeries and I sat with him while he had poison pumped into his body that we hoped would kill the cancer but spare the rest of him. We spent days in the hospital among people trying to do the same thing, and bodies started to look different to me. I had no choice but to reframe my view.

They started to look beautiful. All of them. Even mine. How could I hate these long feet, when they could still carry me through this world? How could I hate this skin that Aaron touched and now my children touch so lovingly? How could this skin house where my soul lives be anything less than a miracle?

Aaron's sickness took and took from his body and pushed *me* into an appreciation of my own. I ran a half marathon. Three of them! Slow as hell, but I did it. And every time my feet hit the pavement, I felt grateful for everything my body could do. I also felt like "Why am I doing this? Thirteen point one miles is way too many. I could be sleeping right now."

This isn't a constant state of being for me. I am still susceptible to the pull of the magnifying mirror in a hotel bathroom, inviting me to inspect my face for wrinkles, blackheads, or a persistent black chin hair that decides to pop up every few months. But often I worship myself the same way that Matthew does. He looks at me like a heart-eyed emoji even when I'm on the third day of stomach flu. He is physically incapable of seeing me and not paying me a compliment. The woman I was in my early twenties would have deflected every compliment he lobbed my way, but the woman I am now says "Thank you." Because I agree with him.

These are things, by the way, I could have always been doing if I weren't so dedicated to trying to trick my body into being a different one. All of those years, when I was definitely not as terribly ugly and deformed as I was sure that I was, I could have instead been happy to be alive and healthy and strong, and out in the world sucking everything I could out of every day. But like my father always told me as I rolled my eyes, youth is wasted on the young.

I'm not wasting any more of my life, or yours, talking about the ways our bodies could be better. The only thing I'm interested in wasting is my Google Photos storage and a few minutes a day, documenting this body I'm so grateful is healthy and is mine.

Chapter Twenty-Four

Options

Alternatives to the word *Stepmom* that we should try to make happen:

Bonus Mom—makes it sound like you were won at the State Fair

~~m(other)~~—works only in print

Other Mother

Alternate Adult

~~Maternal Companion~~—actually, that sounds like a paid position

Mother Figure

Second-Tier Parent

~~Quasi-Mom~~—sounds like a deformity. Nope.

Not Mom—too obvious, and something they could weaponize in
angry moments where you don't want to let them play video
games or whatever

Kinda Mom

Alterna-Mom—nah, makes it sound like I listen to cooler bands
than I actually do

Adjacent Adult

Substitute Parent

Ancillary Adult

Additional Parent

Extra Mom

Supplementary Guardian

Additional Parental Figure—not bad!

Parental Cohort—no.

I'm not saying that Stepmom is the worst thing you can call
a woman who has opted into parenting some children she never
planned on parenting. I'm just saying that maybe we could use an
update? Something that doesn't teach our children to give and receive varying degrees of love based on bloodlines? Doesn't it feel
just a smidge outdated, considering that women can now vote and
own land and even keep our own last names if we'd like to?

Chapter Twenty-Five

All My Children
(I mean this literally, not in reference to the long-running soap opera, so please don't sue me)

My parents were married for over forty years and none of my friends growing up had divorced parents, so I took all my references about this topic from popular culture and fairy tales, and all of those sources will tell you that stepparents are either:

1. Evil or

2. Totally clueless, but well-meaning.

   Stepchildren typically are:

1. Evil or

2. Hateful, resentful little creatures who just want Mom and Dad to get back together.

On my list of Things to Do, "be a stepmom" was nowhere on the list. I could see myself having kids, of course. I could see myself adopting kids. But being a derided quasi-parental figure to children who already *had* two parents? Not super appealing. Becoming a mother is sudden. You don't have a child, and then you do. It's instantaneous. Your child, by birth or otherwise, is yours. You're a mother.

But you don't go from zero to stepmom just by meeting a child, or marrying their parent. It's a process, an evolution. And oh my gosh, what a responsibility. Parenting of any kind, yes, is a huge responsibility. Every time I've left the hospital with a baby (twice), I've walked out thinking, "Are you *sure* I should be taking this kid?" But people expect you to screw up your own kids. The pressure for raising my own babies was high, but not as high as being trusted with someone else's children, particularly because any kid who is getting a stepparent is already coming from a place of loss. The family they knew is gone, and another one is being erected around them. Small things—remembering the right water bottle for soccer practice, getting them signed up for the right camps, getting their doughnut preferences correct—felt huge. These kids had been through enough disappointment in life, I couldn't possibly show up with a chocolate doughnut when the request had been for a chocolate *sprinkle* doughnut!

Matthew felt a similar pressure, but the difference between us—besides that I am at least one inch taller than him—is that my first husband is dead and Matthew's first wife is not. It's their job to co-parent together, and my job to . . . what? Fill in the cracks? We are a somewhat dysfunctional triumvirate of parenthood. I drive carpools and show up to rehearsal, I make dinner and write checks to the soccer club and arrange sleepovers and buy school supplies, but I do not have an official vote in the lives of two children who are the siblings of the children who came out of my body. I can communicate my thoughts and ideas to the two primary parents, but the choices that get made are between the two of them. I am Washington, D.C.—influential, but without official representation.

Often, I think about what I'd be like if my children had a stepmother. In my best fantasies, I would be open and gracious to this other woman. We would forge a fast friendship and work together in perfect harmony to create the best conditions and a happy life for all of us. When people asked about her, I'd say, "Oh, it's just so wonderful that the kids have another loving adult in their lives. You can never have too much love, can you?" The asker would be almost embarrassed to have asked her question. Of *course,* you can't have too much love. Of *course,* the best thing to do is to create an unbreakable alliance with your children's stepmother.

I've seen examples of this kind of relationship in a few of my divorced friends, and in viral "open letters" shared on Facebook: people do it! Moms and stepmoms pose for photos with one another and proclaim their love and appreciation for this woman they never expected to love or appreciate.

In reality? I know that my own heart has two modes: boundlessly loving, and shriveled Grinchiness. So the fact is that I know that I wouldn't always love it if my kids had a stepmom—having someone else there when I was not, tucking them in and shaping their little souls. And I think most of us would probably feel the same way, at least a little bit, at least part of the time. Not because we don't want our children to be loved, but because . . . we want our kids to love us the *most.* It's small and petty and something we'd rather not admit, but there it is.

I am very well aware that I am not Ian or Sophie's mother. I'm aware that while their mother may have chosen not to stay married to Matthew, she also didn't choose to have me enter their lives. My brain knows that they came from a different uterus, but my heart does not. I *love* these kids. As deeply as I love the two that came out of me.

"Is it really as easy as you make it look on Instagram?" someone asked me once about living in our blended family, and I was confused. Do I make it look easy on Instagram? Do I make it look easy in real life? It's as easy as any kind of parenting. Which is to say, there are some days when the entire process of raising a young person is so irritating that I fantasize about getting in my Honda Odyssey alone, turning on a podcast . . . and driving south until I hit the Gulf of Mexico. There are days when I can only handle fifty percent of the kids in any combination, and days when I lock the bathroom door even though I don't have to pee, just so I can have five minutes alone. Far more frequently are the moments where I'm amazed by what we've created as a family, and I want to freeze time and live in the moment forever. Sophie joining Ralph for a game of memory, Baby screaming in delight when Ian walks into his room at daycare, all of them snuggled up in our bed with bowls of popcorn, watching a movie on a Friday night. These are the moments when what we have is so beautiful that I can't believe it can possibly be real.

Parenting is not generally described as easy. Parenting is work. It is an endless checklist of things to do and places to go, and if you can tick off about seventy percent of them by the time the kid is eighteen, you'll have hopefully created a functional adult who will contribute to society. Parenting is work, and so is love. I used to think of that as a negative aspect of love, but it's anything but negative. Love *is* work. It's work that is worth doing. Telling our kids that love is easy and effortless is a disservice to them. Because love challenges us and stretches us. It will help us grow, and if you remember being an adolescent, you know that it hurts to grow.

We do not choose our parents. We do not choose whether their marriages last or when they end. And we do not choose whether or not our parents fall in love again. In short, being a child totally sucks and nothing is in our control. I am well aware that Ian and Sophie did not choose me, and neither did Ralph and Baby. They are all in the same boat when it comes to having a well-meaning but sometimes hapless woman at the helm of the family. These kids have seen love die, and seen love grow, and I want them all to know that love is a choice that we make and a job that we do. We choose each other every day. Even when things are hard, even when we are hurt.

Loving these kids means loving their mother, and being grateful for her existence, even when we are not on speaking terms. It means recognizing and remembering that I picked this life, and this love, the same way I picked Aaron and the same way I picked Matthew. I've stepped into this life, as a mom, as a stepmom. I'm still walking, stepping lightly, often tripping, sometimes falling.

Is it as easy as it looks on Instagram? Yes. And no. But it's so damn worth it.

Chapter Twenty-Six

Sad and Lucky

People always imply that being with me must be hard for Matthew. They start out with a weird compliment like "he's a saint . . . he's such a good guy" and segue quickly into the casual "so . . . how does he deal with it?" *It* being my dead husband.

I imagine they're thinking he is jealous of the love I had before, that he's uncomfortable with my grief, bitter over his second-place finish in the competition of Who Nora Loves Most. He's not. He's not in second place, though people assume that he's a runner-up, and he's not uncomfortable with my grief. Trust me, I ask him all the time and I know when he's lying because he does this weird thing when he is even *thinking* about being less than truthful.

"I feel really guilty sometimes," I admitted to Matthew one night.

Periodically, I respond to a loving gesture from my husband by reminding Matthew that I am still in love with Aaron. I'm not just reminding *him*, I'm reminding myself: it's a reflex, an automatic defense of Aaron, and of my life with him.

That particular night, Matthew had put a record on my record player. "Aaron gave that to me," I said, "the whole box set. For no reason. He just knew I liked Bright Eyes and he got me every single record." I said this in a way that was more accusatory than informative. Matthew responded with more kindness than I would have, but I could tell I hadn't improved the mood in the house. When the record stopped playing, he didn't turn it over.

My admission of guilt felt like I was confessing to a crime I'd been carrying around for decades, not just a year or so.

"Same," said Matthew.

Matthew feels sad that Aaron is dead and sad that Ralph lost his father and sad that I lost my husband and Mae Mae lost her son and Nikki lost her brother. He feels lucky he found me, lucky to be in Ralph's life, lucky to have four kids who are healthy and happy (knock on wood).

We are both trying to find our footing in this new life we built, and we both know that we built this life with the wreckage of our old ones. Matthew's old life lives just a half mile from us. We see her at soccer games and our relationship could be categorized anywhere between "complicated" and "next question, please." Nobody tells me that I'm a *saint* for being with Matthew, or for raising his children with him. Whatever the fairy tales told us about being rescued by a man was false. Women have always been our own heroes. Beast needed Belle in order to turn back into a human man (which was also a mistake because I am not the only person who thinks that cartoon beast is hot, and I know it). Prince Eric would have drowned at sea if it weren't for Ariel. We rescue broken guys like they're stray dogs. We love them for the fact that they're missing an eyeball or only have three legs. I realize that I might be taking the rescue dog/rescue man analogy too far, but let's just go with it.

Matthew, by the way, *is* a saint and is a good guy, but not because he dared to enter a relationship with me. He's a good guy because he's principled in everything he does. He loves me, and he loves Aaron. He has to love Aaron. Aaron is why he has me. Not just because Aaron died, although not having a living husband did make it easier to date Matthew. But because Aaron's love and Aaron's death created the Nora I am right now.

On my Best Life days, I feel so grateful for a beating heart and a functional body that nothing else could possibly matter. But anyone who lives a hundred percent in their Best Life mode is either Oprah or . . . end of list.

Many days, I'm not so sure about this Nora. The other Nora was awesome. She could throw a baby shower while nursing a baby and a sick husband. She could host brunch every Sunday and manage a chemo schedule. She made her own granola bars because she didn't want her husband to get *more* cancer from some unknown cancer-causing additive in some mass-market granola bar. She took things a little too far in that respect. She showed up dressed and made up for everything from a brain surgery to a baptism. The version of me that Matthew got is slower and messier. She barely grocery shops, let alone cooks. She showers only when absolutely necessary. She's fine, I guess.

I've worried, since I met Matthew, that there's just nothing in this relationship for him. What does he get out of being with this second-rate version of me?

Ernest Hemingway wrote "the world breaks everyone, and afterward, many are stronger in the broken places."

The world does break everyone—that is a damn guarantee. The world breaks everyone, and everything. Families are snapped apart by death, money, drugs, divorce, the wrong thing said at the wrong time to the wrong sibling who will never let it go. Many of us are stronger at the broken places, but many of us are just . . . broken. Not that you'd ever know it. We humans are experts at hiding our broken parts. We love to pull ourselves up by the bootstraps. We absolutely insist that whatever didn't kill us made us stronger, even if it's all we can do to get ourselves out of bed in the morning. The broken places are scary, so we do our best to cover them up with big smiles and expensive handbags and well-lit Instagram posts.

Finding real, lasting, big romantic love is a miracle. Think of all the people in the world. Right off the bat, most are dumb or annoying. The ones who aren't dumb or annoying may not be in your age range, or live on your continent, may not speak your language, may not be single! The fact of finding a person you can love and be loved by is truly a remarkable event, and if you are in love right now, I want you to put this book down and turn to your beloved, or call them on the phone, or send them a text, or if it's a hundred years in the future just hologram into their brains and tell them "I am so very glad I found you."

Our holiday cards went out in late January this year. They feature gorgeous photographs of our beaming children, my current husband and me sitting in the grass after our backyard wedding. We chose a selection of photos not because it was hard to choose from the photographs our friend Nicole snapped on our wedding day, but because we didn't get a photo of all of us together. Not one. The cards we sent out remind the recipient of our children's names and ages and wish them a happy (non-denominational) holiday season. They do not tell you that this beautiful family of ours was built from the parts of other families, but that is how we got here, on this holiday card that I didn't get around to mailing until well after any related holiday.

And even though I sometimes think Matthew got a pretty

down-market version of me, he's *into* this Nora. He thinks she's so great he agreed to spend the rest of his life with her. Yes, he has low standards.

Of course we are lucky. Both of us. We are lucky to have come through with broken parts, to have survived. We are lucky to have found each other, even though all of that luck is tinged with a little bit of sadness. We both know it. And we both need reminding sometimes. Sometimes we need the other person to flip the record over, or to change it entirely.

If I squint hard enough, I can start to see what Matthew sees in me.* Which is that I have been in love like this before. I know what it means to promise 'til death do us part, and to follow through on that promise. Anyone can do that, though. But I'm willing to do it *twice*. This new family of ours is not a consolation prize for what I lost, but it consoles me nonetheless. Ralph, nearly five, draws a photo at school, each person a collection of circles and lines. His teacher carefully labels each amoeba-like outline: Mama, Dad, Dad, Brother, Brother, Sister. A stranger at the grocery store tells Sophie she looks just like me, and her face freezes somewhere between "that's not my mom!" and "thanks?" Christmas comes, and no matter where The Bigs spend it, they are leaving their family to be with . . . their family.

These four kids of ours know that love has real power, but it is not all-powerful. Our family crest will be six broken hearts with a tattered banner beneath it reading:

Sad and lucky.

---

* It would be easier to just ask him, but he's in the other room with noise-canceling headphones on.

Chapter Twenty-Seven

Dear _____

I n a little over a year, my family experienced exponential growth through both a significant merger and via organic growth. That's my business way of saying "Oh my GOSH I have the four kids I always wanted!" Before I had kids, I had a lot of ideas of the kind of parent I would be, and I became the epitome of everything I once looked down on (Bob Stroller, Honda Odyssey, often running late, forgetting it was pajama day, visiting the McDonald's drive-thru more than I care to admit).

I came from a family of four, and we were all obsessed with our parents' scoreboard. It was, as far as I know, imaginary, but we were always striving to claw our way to the top. Parenting is glorious and glory-less. It is hard and humbling, and I really wouldn't trade it for anything. I know now that for all the ways I resented my parents, they were just doing their best at a hard and thankless job. There are no perfect parents. Mostly, we're all kinda failures, actually. Once you realize that even the best parents sometimes look at their kids and think "Why am I doing this?", it takes a lot of the pressure off. Seriously, even the people who look like really good parents on Instagram have dropped a phone on their baby's head while playing Candy Crush or missed their kid's goal in soccer because they were checking their email or even plain-old forgotten to pick up their kid from daycare. These are all examples of things I have done and also things I tell myself that other people have done, okay? But most of us—even me—are trying our best.

Everyone in the world wants to feel special and known and seen. It's very challenging to make someone feel special when you have fifteen minutes between soccer practices and you can't find the baby's shoe and the dog just peed on the floor and you still don't know what you're eating for dinner later.

For all their many shortcomings, to be documented in another book at some time, my parents were excellent letter-writers. I have beautiful missives from each of them, written not just for milestones but for no reason at all other than they were thinking about me, noticing me, and seeing me.

Each of the following letters was written for and given to our children long before this book was written. I asked each of them if I could publish them, and received their permission. Baby and Ralph were obviously not that into either the asking part or the permission part, but if they grow up and hate that these letters are in the world, it will make some therapist a very wealthy woman.

It may feel a little bit silly, or a little bit odd, or a little bit like *who has time for this kinda stuff,* but if you want someone in your life to feel just how loved and seen they are? Write them a letter.

Chapter Twenty-Eight

Dear Ralphie

TO: Ralph, Age 4 and 3/4

FROM: Mom, AKA Nora

RE: Your dead dad and other stuff

November 25, 2017

Dear Ralph,

I still don't know how to spend your dad's deathaversary. We haven't had that many of them, but I was hoping that some clear tradition would emerge. That the day would always be holy and sanctified and reserved for quiet reflection and prayer and crying. That a group of doves would materialize, just waiting to be released into a clear blue sky. But it's just a day. For all the ways our lives were changed on November 25, it's just one of 365 days in a year, a day that holds meaning for just a handful of people. I wake up today to texts from friends asking regular people questions like "What is the name of that podcast you told me to listen to?" and "Are we meeting on Thursday or nah?" Not super-special grief day questions like "How are you reflecting on the love of your dead husband today, sweet Nora?" Nobody texts you, because you are only 4 and ¾. That ¾ is very important to you.

The summer after your dad died, our family met up to execute his final wishes: becoming a part of the Rum River, the site for his idyllic childhood summers and for his debaucherous parties in high school, college, and adulthood until he got cancer. There were two locations for Aaron's ashes to spend eternity: the hobby farm his grandfather bought in the seventies, and Auntie Robbin's country house, both located on the Mighty Rum, which zigzags from Lake Mille Lacs until it joins up with the lesser-known Mississippi. Your dad *loved* the Rum River. His actual request was to have a Viking funeral on the Rum, but permits wouldn't allow us to shoot a flaming arrow into a canoe holding his cadaver, so instead we turned him into magic dust and brought him to the place he loved.

The ashes of a person are not like the ashes you find in a fireplace. They are gritty, sandy, a little bit sparkly. Your dad was stylish, and was cremated in his favorite J. Crew outfit, with his favorite Nikes on. So the grains that rolled through our fingers are not just his flesh and bones, I know that. In the end, even with our Nikes on, we fit into two small plastic bags.

I don't know what I expected ashes to do in water, but they didn't float away, they clumped together, and bloomed into a cloud. They stayed there, right in front of us, swirling between the rocks we stood on when the water was low. I licked the rest of him from my fingers, to make him a part of me.

But he is always a part of me. A part of us. I see your dad in your eyes, and the way they change from hazel to bright green with your outfits and your moods. I see him in your skinny legs and the way you cross them when you're concentrating. Your dad is everywhere. When you were tiny, you told me that he was the sky and the grass and the trees. Sometimes you'd stand on your little picnic table and wave at the sky. "Hey, Papa!" you'd call out to the clouds above.

You were not yet two when your dad died. Your memories of him are really just my memories of him, filtered through my brain and my eyes. I do my best to make your dad a part of our lives. Not just yours and mine, but our whole family's. Aaron's portrait hangs in our living room. Aaron's art is on our walls. Aaron's birthday and our wedding anniversary are on our calendar. When a song reminds me of Aaron, I turn it up and tell everyone why it's important to me. When a funny memory pops into my head, I tell everyone the story. The Bigs know anecdotes about Aaron. They know how he lost his first job (falling through the roof at the movie theater), they know his dance moves (knee wiggle, shoulder shimmy), and they know what he made fun of me for (not knowing anything cool, picking my nose, leaving cabinet doors open, not putting the lids on things). They never met Aaron, but they know him. You know him. You know his favorite color (red). You know when I'm missing him. You never once saw your dad slide on his knees across the dance floor just to make me laugh, but the other day, standing in the kitchen, you shouted, "Hey, Mom!" And did just that.

Your father was a non-renewable resource, and there is a part of me that is miserly about his death. That wants to keep it packaged up just for the two of us, a symbol of our apartness from the rest of the world. We are all that is left of that family of three, the only two who went through the dark together. Your dad's deathaversary feels like a day that is just for us, so today I packed you into the minivan, kissed Matthew and the rest of the kids good-bye, and headed up to the Rum River. On the way, we picked up Moe and Bronson. They never met Aaron, but they have a dead dad/husband, too, so they get a pass. We stopped at McDonald's for Happy Meals, and at the junk store where your dad would wander the aisles, trying to find the funniest purchase possible.

I don't know what I expected us to do when we got to the river, but Auntie Robbin gave us her country house for the day, and the four of us settled in. We sat in the living room and watched two mama deer try to cross the river with their babies. We walked into the woods, crunching through the fallen leaves, howling like wolves and screaming, "I LOVE YOU, PAPA! I LOVE YOU, AARON!"

Most often, when you speak, it's like a typical child. We hear a lot of butt jokes, a lot of poop talk. And sometimes, it is like you are a small oracle sent to guide me through this life. Today you were walking ahead of me, the cold November sun fading in the late afternoon. "Mom," you called out to me, "follow me! I'm here to show you the way to God."

It turns out you were showing me the way to a ravine you almost fell into while wearing Crocs. Almost-five-year-olds are subpar navigators.

There isn't much to do at the river in November, so we packed up our stuff and headed back home just before the rush hour. You and Bronson fell asleep in the backseat of the van, and Moe and I listened to Aaron's favorite songs.

I didn't know enough to expect something this good for us, Ralph. A part of me thought that it would be the two of us, always. A little island, a little club that was not accepting new members. But you, like your father, have always been a person to sow love. When you were really little, and Papa was sick, we took you with us everywhere, even the oncology center. Papa spent two nights a month there, and we would go to visit him. You were just learning to walk, and you would go from room to room, quietly and sweetly, always gravitating toward the people who were suffering most, the ones with the fewest visitors. You have the ability to sense where love is needed, and to shine it in that direction.

Your nearly-five-year-old heart knows that Matty Daddy isn't a replacement for Papa Aaron. They exist in the same family. Both have a huge impact on who you are. It's nature and nurture, working together. As much as I see Aaron in you, I see Matthew, too. You've picked up on his mannerisms, and his catchphrases, especially "Guys! Come on, I'm going to be late to work!"

Right now, your father is a mystery to you, an abstraction. That will change with the years, I know. You will have days when you miss him so much it hurts, days when his absence is palpable to you, and days when it all seems like something that must have happened to someone else.

Tonight you are sleeping next to me in my bed, with your Matty Daddy and Baby and our dumb dog. The Bigs are snoozing in their rooms down the hallway. I am watching your chest rise and fall, and your small hand resting on top of my arm.

You were right, today. Whether it's the way to God, to happiness, to love . . . you are here to show me the way.

xoxo,
Mom

Chapter Twenty-Nine

Dear Baby

TO: Baby, Age 1-ish
FROM: Your Mom (whose name you refuse to say)
RE: Sorry for not wanting you, but it was complicated

Dear Baby,

Man, when you grow up and read this book you're gonna have a lot of questions. One of them is probably going to be, "Okay, wait . . . you didn't want me?"

It's not like I didn't want *you*. I didn't want any baby. That doesn't sound much better. I wanted you a *lot*. But I was afraid to want you. Your uncle Dave once told me that wanting is risking. To love something, or want something, is to risk disappointment. To risk our own pain.

And I'd had a lot of pain. I'd lost my dad, I'd lost Ralph's dad, I'd lost another baby, Ralph's little sibling, right before my dad and husband died. And I thought if I wanted you, I'd jinx it. You'd die, and it wouldn't just hurt *me,* it would hurt Ian and Sophie and Ralph and your dad.

I could handle my own pain, but I couldn't handle theirs.

They weren't scared at all, by the way. They were ready for you. They loved you right away, so much that actually, it sometimes annoyed you, and you'd push away their faces and say "no kiss!"

One time, an intuitive healer at a craft fair told me that you were a healing force, a light for our family. And I kind of believed her. I kind of thought that sounded like a lot of pressure to put on a small person. But Baby, you *are.*

It didn't matter that Sophie wanted a sister; the moment she walked into the room, she loved you. She and Ian both held you and cried happy tears and even though you'd had a really long day, being born and all, you looked at them with big, wide eyes.

Ralph was mostly interested in the big TV in the hospital room, but he warmed up to you later. When you cry in your car seat, Ralph will pretend to punch himself in the face, just because it brings you joy. I hope this doesn't mean you're a serial killer.

We all came from different places, but this is the only family you'll ever know. This is your normal—three different families all whipped into one. But this is the family you were born into, and you made it feel so simple.

I wish I could say that I realized it the moment you were born, and I instantly fell in love with you and realized that you *were* the light for our family. But you will eventually be able to read or download a podcast and you'll be able to read this book and know the truth. It was hard to love you, because it was hard for me to be happy. You were born in a month where I lost a lot, and that sadness settled in and got comfortable.

The presence of your beautiful new life, in this beautiful new family, seemed in such contrast to the depth of what I had lost, and what I still missed. I felt bad. And I felt bad for feeling bad. I felt bad for not giving you the joyful welcome you deserved, and because of all the versions of Nora that had ever existed, that this is what you and Ian and Sophie and Dad and Ralphie got. I sometimes felt like you guys got majorly ripped off.

In America, they send you home twenty-four hours after you expel a human from your body, and you just kinda fend for yourself. I didn't just have my blanket of sadness, I had you, and a busted-up body, and a bunch of hormones racing through my bloodstream. Your dad and I don't really argue, but two days after I'd given birth, I was sitting in an adult diaper filled with my own blood, and I was sad and mad. Madame and Shar Bear hadn't come by the house yet, and I was upset. Didn't they care about you? About me? Shouldn't they each be playing the role of Elated Grandmother, holding and rocking you so I could just get some damn sleep? Somehow, this was Dad's fault, of course, and when I suggested this he looked at me like I was made out of centipedes, which made me madder. And then he left the room and I put a pillow over my face and cried.

And then Mae Mae showed up. She was excited to meet you, but also a little sad. You didn't mean to be, but you're a symbol of how life continues after death takes the people we love. Ralph's dad was her baby, and you are my baby with Matthew. And over the past two years, she and I had struggled with how to fit ourselves together without our main puzzle piece. But you were what bridged that gulf between us. You snuggled into her and slept while she and I said everything we hadn't said for the past two years, while we cried all the tears we'd been saving up. She'd been afraid that she wouldn't fit into our new family, but of course she did. She's your grandma. And Ralph and Sophie and Ian's grandma, too. She's my mother-in-law, just like Matthew's mother is. She is a part of our family, forever. A part of my heart, forever. Your very existence has bonded all of us—all of these different families—together forever. And all you had to do was show up.

All of this letter is about how you make other people feel, and what you do for other people. That's partially because you're only a year old, so we're still getting to know you. I can't write a whole chapter about how you won't eat vegetables (but seriously, you won't, and I worry you're gonna get scurvy or some other old-timey disease).

They call babies like you Rainbow Babies, the beauty after the storm of infant or pregnancy loss. Your nickname is Baby, because StormtrooperLuckyCharm is . . . lengthy? We tried to call you Stormy, but then a Kardashian copied us. It's fine, though, because even as a nickname, it doesn't suit you at all. That intuitive healer was right about you. You're not just a rainbow; you're a light. You can't help but shine.

Love you,

Nora (AKA Mom. It's just as easy as saying Dad so I don't know what you're getting at pretending you can't say it.*)

---

* Turns out, you just had a ton of ear infections and couldn't hear us at all! You've since gotten ear tubes and have said a lot more words, including "Mom." Sorry, dude!

Chapter Thirty

Dear Sophie

TO: Sophie, Age 11

FROM: Your Nora

RE: Which kid do I love most?

December 24, 2017

Dear Sophie,

Tonight we held hands while we walked into church together. Me, a Catholic who has turned to the bland side (Lutheranism). You, a child who grew up without religion, who chooses to tag along with me from time to time. Probably for the free cookies.

You turned to me in the parking lot and said, "You know what I was thinking about yesterday?" and I shook my head. "I was thinking," you continued, "about how you must love Ralph more than me. And how you always will. Because he's yours."

That was . . . NOT what I would have guessed. Yesterday was Christmas Eve eve. I thought for sure you'd have been thinking about whether or not we'd bought you the $95 leggings you asked for (we did not). I squeezed your hand and thanked you for telling me that, and we walked into the warmth of the church, together.

We had an hour together, just the two of us. An hour of music and stories about a God who did the impossible: who got a girl pregnant, convinced her fiancé *not* to have her stoned to death, and then became the baby inside of her. The reason for the season, ya know? At the end, we held hands with the rest of the congregation. We lit candles and held them up in the darkness of the church, hundreds of tiny flames illuminating this vast space.

I don't know if you remember any of our conversation, but I will remember it forever.

For a long time, love felt like something that I had to earn, that could be taken from me at any time for bad behavior. It felt like just above my head there was a gauge that only I could sense. The gauge measured how much love I received from the people around me. If I was good, more love poured in, and the gauge moved up. If I was bad, the love poured out, the gauge went down. Love was subject to change, based on my behavior. The better I was, the more I got: from God, my parents, my siblings, my friends. It felt like any love I didn't get went to someone else, someone who deserved it more. Someone who didn't yell at their little brother or forget to return library books for months or lose her goggles at the pool.

Notice I said that it *felt* that way. Like you, I am a middle child. A deep feeler, a keen observer, prone to letting anger simmer inside me before unleashing it on the unsuspecting.

Everything growing up is a zero-sum game: there is a winner, and there is a loser. You learn this in school and in sports, and it's not always wrong. There is not enough of everything to go around, so when someone gets more, it means someone else is getting less. I'd say "it's simple math," but I've seen your math homework and I don't think that phrase applies anymore. This idea of love— that it could only go so far, that there was only so much of it—was simple, and easy to understand, and made love hard and scary for me. If love could be earned, it could also be taken away. The God who loved me and saw the good in me also saw the bad in me, the sin in me. The parents who loved me unconditionally could also get angry with me, withdraw from me. If I fell in love, and the other person didn't, then what? If I loved someone, and the person died, what then? The love would be gone, I guess. The gauge would go down.

Neither of us expected to be here, Sophie. A few years ago, you lived in a little blue house with your mom and your dad and your big brother. You didn't know what was happening, but you knew *something* was happening, that the fabric that held your life together was sprouting holes and falling apart. And when it did, your dad did his best to patch things up and make a new life for the three of you, and your mom did her best as well. Tomorrow, you'll wake up in a house with your father and me, your big brother, your little brother, and your little-little brother. You went from the youngest to the middle, from one of two to one of four. From two parents to three parents.

A few years ago, I lived in a little green house with my husband Aaron and our baby, Ralph. Aaron was so sick, and I knew he would die soon. I was afraid for me, afraid for Ralph. Aaron's love was my first taste of real life magic. His love was easy and pure. I didn't have to do anything or be anything special besides my flawed self, and he loved me anyway. Without Aaron, what would I be? Who would love me?

The last few weeks of his life were hard. I saw how easy it was for people to conflate love and possession: how desperately they confused their needs with his. It felt like the last two weeks of his life were spent watching the people who loved him try to claim their piece of him before it was too late. It made me sad and tired and desperate, like I needed to do the same. Nobody, I thought, loved him as much as I did. If you lined all our loves up, sorted them by height or weight or general good looks, mine would win. My love was the best love. Does that sound silly? It should.

I was with Aaron when he died. He was with me, and then he was not, and for a brief moment, everything in the world made perfect sense to me: I saw the universe, and myself, and my place in the cosmos. And then, that little peephole slammed shut and I was back on Earth. Back in our little green house. I was sad, and I was scared and I was angry. I was thirty-one years old, and my Big Love was dead. My heart was dead. That was that. I took the love I had and I wrapped it around Ralph and me like a thick layer of bubble wrap that could protect us from ever being hurt again. It felt safe and also lonely.

And then your dad happened. I thought I was just going to Moe's to burn some stuff in a bonfire. I didn't think I was going to meet another Big Love. I didn't think that I would love someone again. I didn't think I would love a whole bunch of someones again. And a part of me didn't even *want* to. I felt defensive of Aaron, and of me and Ralph. How could I love your dad, and you kids, if I also loved Aaron and Ralph? How could I love my old life *and* a new life? I didn't have enough love to spread it that far, so why even try?

Here is what nobody told me as a kid. Not in church, not at home. We have enough love to go around. We don't always have enough clean towels, or Coca-Cola in those cute little bottles, or milk, but we have enough love. We have enough for everyone, and from everyone.

Don't confuse love with time, or attention, or anything else that can be quantified. Trying to measure it will never make you happier, will never give you a satisfying answer.

For millions of years, people have been trying to define love, and every definition is inadequate and unsatisfying, but I know what love is not: it is not something that runs out, it is not something we hold over one another, or against one another. The only secret about love that you really need to know is that even when you feel like you've worn it out or used it all up, it's always, always in your power to make more. Love is the truest magic we do for one another. There is no potion or spell for it, there is just the dazzling act of choosing to be there for one another, over and over again. On days when you step on one of Ralph's LEGOs. On days when Ian pretends not to hear you when you ask for a refill of your drink. On days when the baby is sick, Ian has soccer, Ralph hasn't taken a nap, and the dog has chewed up your favorite pen.

I don't love Ralphie more than you, Soph. I love him differently, because the two of you are different people, and I am different people to you. I am not your biological mother and you did not come out of my body, but I am yours and you are mine and we are all each other's. Because our two broken worlds collided and made this one: a bizarro little planet where we all have different last names but remarkably similar noses for people with limited shared DNA.

Love is not Coca-Cola in the cute glass bottles. It isn't the middle seat in the van or the last Chipotle chip. Love is different.

There is no more or most, except in this context: the more

people you love, the more love you have. And love, even the annoying, messy kind from your brothers, is the most important thing we have.

Love,
Nora

Chapter Thirty-One

Dear Ian

TO: Ian, age 16
FROM: Your Nora
RE: The Sex Talk

Dear Ian,

Just kidding! This is not a sex talk. Your dad and I will save
that for our college visits, when you are a captive audience in a
rental car.

Yesterday, you asked me why I believe in God.

You were struggling through a particularly grueling theology
assignment at your new Catholic high school, after being raised for
sixteen years without any religion. You'd just found out days before
that Jesus was the son of GOD, and you looked at me with concern,
as if I'd just told you that my birth mother was a Volvo station
wagon.

Hearing it through your ears, it did sound a little . . .

preposterous, I guess? But I reminded you that you aren't at that school to learn what to *believe*, you were there to learn *how* to learn, and to be open to what other people hold dear to them.

Youth is wasted on the young, and often, so is education. Your assignments, I know, are often a mere distraction from your life's calling to play soccer and watch Snapchat messages. I know that I had similar feelings about school, though I now look longingly at your textbooks and think, "If only my biggest concern was a five-paragraph paper about the Industrial Revolution." Then I think, "When was the Industrial Revolution again?" And I'm glad to have my own concerns.

Having a high schooler in my house has offered me proof that I have indeed gotten progressively stupider with every passing day since I earned my diploma. It has also offered me a front-row seat to the promise and capabilities of your generation. It gives me hope. No pressure.

Back to your question and your theology homework. Certainly, I should be able to help you with a *theology* assignment. Except not. Your paper was about the Catechism, and while you weren't looking, I Googled it on my phone because I had absolutely no idea what that word meant. I'll save you the time: Catechism is a collection of questions and answers meant to teach people about Christianity—specifically, about Catholicism. You repeated the assignment aloud to me for the second time. You were to choose a part of the Catechism and write a response to it. Your options:

God invites us into a personal relationship with him.

There is proof of God's love for us.

We all yearn for connection with God.

Your issue was that you didn't believe in any of these statements and that they all sounded insane.

I could offer you no help with the Catechism, which was slightly embarrassing because I went to the very same Catholic high school you are now attending. In fact, after attending eight years of Catholic elementary school, and then attending four years of Catholic college, how did I not know what Catechism meant?

Because it all sounded insane to me, too. The only thing I remember about my formal religious education is it sliding directly off me. In high school, I learned to take notes, to find the essential points of any text and write to them. I did not learn to believe in God, or to love God. I did not learn how to spot Grace, or God's mercy. I heard a lot of antiquated words, like Catechism. But I did not think that God loved me, or anyone else for that matter. I thought of God as a mostly disinterested force. An absentee Father who may show up for a volleyball game or two.

My life, through that point, had been very easy. I mean, very easy. My parents were in love. We had enough—or, if we didn't, my parents hid the truth from us very well—I didn't have to think about much, because everything was provided for me. None of this was proof of God. It was proof of . . . my parents' luck and my own privilege.

Why, you repeated, did I believe in God?

I remember *trying* to explain it to you, and realizing that you had already glazed over and checked out, and I could have said "because one time I saw the face of Jesus in a hot dog and he told me that if I ate him I could have eternal life" and you wouldn't have noticed.

What I want to say to you now, is this: I believe in God now, but not because of Catechism. Not because of what someone told me, or an essay I had to write for credit. I believe in God because I see

God every day. I see God in people. I feel God in people. God is *not* a disinterested Father. God is love. She is air. God is seeing you carry Ralph to the car after your soccer games, in the wrinkling of your baby brother's nose when you make him smile, in the story of you covering your little sister's ears so she didn't hear your mom and dad fighting when you were both so little.

God is in the good parts, and the hard parts. Because life is *hard*, and that's not a newsflash for you. Your childhood was not easy. You learned at a young age how to cover up for the pain around you, how to smooth the rough edges and not make a fuss. You learned how to make up for the shortcomings of the adults around you. We all suffer. We all die. We're all loved. By each other and by an unseen force that I call God, but you could just as easily choose to call it Brenda. It's not a love we have to earn; it's a love that is just there. And it shows up in one another. It shows up in you and Sophie calling Ralph your little brother without even being asked to. It shows up in your dad and me, meeting when we'd both had our lives destroyed.

God is not a promise that life will be easy. God is a promise that we will all experience joy and shattering pain. But we are *here*. We get all of this. We get each other. We have each other—this family—because everything we once thought was stable fell apart.

Even then, God was there. Even now.

I believe in God because of you, and our family. Believe in God, or don't. Either way, dude, you are loved.

xoxo,

Nora

Chapter Thirty-Two

Feminist Agenda

THE FEMINIST AGENDA (ACCORDING TO INSECURE MEN)

12:00 A.M.–6:00 A.M. Devil worship and blood rituals

6:00–7:00 Tend to armpit hair; eschew showering and basic hygiene

7:00–8:00 Feed and tend to large pack of cats

8:00–9:00 Invent wage gap

9:00–9:30 Breakfast: conflict-free eggs freely given by a gender-fluid chicken

9:00–10:00 Fabricate statistics on sexual assault

10:00–11:00 Get a recreational abortion

11:00–12:00 Conspire to take jobs away from white men

12:00–1:00 P.M. Lunch, probably something gluten-free and vegan

1:00–3:00 Conference call with other underrepresented groups of females hell-bent on destroying the mythological "patriarchy"

3:00–4:00 Delete the Second Amendment and take away all the guns

4:00–5:00 Destroy traditional marriage

6:00–7:00 Assault family values by creating a safe place for non-traditional families of all kinds

7:00–8:00 Dinner of fair-trade, organic, ethically raised vegetables

8:00–12:00 Netflix

THE ASPIRATIONAL FEMINIST AGENDA

5:30 A.M. Wake up; remain woke for remainder of day

5:30–6:30 Work out, listening to playlist personally curated by Beyoncé and Gloria Steinem. Focus on arms, to lift up women of color and non-gender-conforming individuals. Shoulders, for future generations to stand on. Butt, for yourself, not for the male gaze.

6:30–7:30 Write inspiring article about female representation in media. Read literally none of the comments. Not even one.

7:30–8:00 Meditation with healing crystals

8:00–9:00 Close the wage gap

9:00–5:00 P.M. Smash the glass ceiling

5:00–6:00 Conference call with intersectional group of underrepresented individuals on how best to smash the patriarchy and achieve a more equitable world.

6:00 Dinner

7:00–10:00 Netflix

MY ACTUAL FEMINIST AGENDA

Wake up to coffee my husband made (good boy).

Do my best to not raise buttheads.

Do my best not to be a butthead.

Netflix.

Chapter Thirty-Three

Big, Gross, Angry Feminist

I had no interest in becoming a feminist. Feminism was for mean, gross, angry women who hated men, and I was not that kind of woman. First off, I wasn't a woman. I was a girl. Sure, I was biologically an adult woman, but the word *woman* wasn't as appealing as the word *girl*. I was a girl. A girl who liked boys, and a girl who wanted boys to like her, too. You can't like boys if you hate men, and all feminists hated men. The feminists at my college were always complaining about things like women's rights and birth control and the monologues of vaginas. What rights were they so concerned with? I had no idea. We had lots of rights! Nobody was outright oppressing us! We could vote! We could hold elected office! I mean, there weren't a whole lot of us in executive-level positions, and none of us had ever been president, but that didn't mean the world was a sexist place. Only that the right woman hadn't come along yet. So far, we were all just duds, I guess. The Feminists planned a Take Back the Night rally that was little more than an inconvenience because it made it harder for us to catch a campus shuttle to a party where we would drink warm beer and laugh at unfunny jokes made by dumb boys. Plus, why did we need a rally against rape? None of us were getting pulled into the bushes and raped by strangers! Several of our friends had sex they didn't want to have in the basements of house parties when they were blackout drunk, but we didn't say the R word. Instead, we followed the lead of our Alpha female and shunned our friend for a few weeks, our silent treatment the only appropriate punishment for her "sloppiness."

As you can see, I had no need for feminism in 2004!

All of the above was painful to write, and painful to read, and painfully true for more than just me and the women I went to college with. A lot of us came of age believing that feminism was useless and outdated, and probably most importantly, the kind of thing that guys wouldn't like. We knew, from a very young age, that one of our roles is to keep everyone comfortable, always at the expense of our own comfort.

When Aaron was first diagnosed with brain cancer, it seemed so outlandish. So unique and shocking. But I started to notice that brain cancer was actually *everywhere*. Everyone knew someone with brain cancer, or who had died of brain cancer. It was an epidemic, and I said as much to Aaron's doctor. He had been studying brain cancer since before I was born and disagreed. There wasn't more brain cancer now, not really. It's just that I notice it now. He compared it to when you purchase a new car. The car feels special when you buy it, but once you get it on the road, or into a parking lot, you see them everywhere. I nodded skeptically. Brain cancer is like my Honda Accord?

Dr. Mustache, as we called him behind his back, was totally right. Brain cancer opens your eyes. I wasn't seeing something new,

I was seeing something that was always there, but that I'd been able to ignore because it didn't affect me directly.

The word *privilege* makes a lot of people feel gross and weird. It made *me* feel gross and weird and so I avoided it and rejected it. How dare you say I am privileged? You don't know what my life is like! Well, you do know what my life is like, because I tell you about it all the time, but acknowledging your own privilege is not saying that your life isn't hard, or your problems aren't real. It is and they are. Acknowledging your privilege is just like me noticing brain cancer. It's opening yourself and your awareness up to the experiences of others, experiences that have always been there, but that you didn't notice. To things that may not negatively affect you directly, but that you can and should still care about.

My feminist awakening was not 0 to 60. It was a gradual opening of my eyes and ears to the buzzing of the alarm I'd been sleeping through. It was noticing how my male colleagues consistently talked over the women in the room, and how the women always brought in coffee and snacks for everyone. It was having a male friend I trusted tell me my salary requirement for a job I was interviewing for should be $20K less than what he made for the same job at a similar company. It was looking around me and the industry I worked in at the time and realizing that all the faces at the table were *white* and *most were male*. It was listening and believing the women of color who said they were being paid even less than white ladies, who pointed out that it's hard to lean in to a table where you don't even have a seat. Feminism isn't just realizing how a male-dominated society has impacted me, but how it's benefited me, too. Because being a white, middle-class lady *does* have its benefits, and they aren't benefits I've earned, either.

My mother and I have different interpretations of what it means to be a feminist, and sometimes that makes me incredibly mad. But she's had twice as long as I have had to soak up the detrimental effects of a world that values women less than men. "The patriarchy will dismantle *itself* eventually," she said to me once, as if any great power structure has ever willingly opened its gates to a more equitable way of life. The patriarchy won't dismantle itself, and it won't be dismantled by angry Facebook posts and tweet storms, but that doesn't stop me from doing both of those things and then hating myself for it! It will be changed by what we teach this next generation of kids. Our kids have gone to marches and campaign rallies. They have door-knocked. They know where we donate our money, and why.

Much to my disappointment, both the children who came out of my body are boys. I'm aware of the awesome responsibility of raising all four of them to dismantle a patriarchy that is hurting all of them, and benefitting all of them. I have four middle-class white kids! What the world around us needs is for them to understand the ways their skin and their economic status work to their advantage, and all the reasons why that is total bullcrap.

In the words of Amy Grant, it takes a little time, sometimes, to get the *Titanic* turned back around. That's an unfortunate lyric, given the fate of the *Titanic*. And I think it's also a poor excuse for complacency. Things change when people care enough to change them, and people can change, when they care to.

I'm not a girl anymore. I'm a woman now. And a big, gross, angry feminist.

Chapter Thirty-Four

Destroy the Patriarchy After You Propose to Me

Proposal stories fall into the same category as birth stories, dream stories, and drunk stories: we only care about them if they're about us.

But listen: Matthew's proposal was *terrible*.

We're married, so it got the job done, but just barely.

And it's not because my expectations were too high, because my last proposal was *me* proposing to Aaron while he lay in a hospital bed, newly diagnosed with a brain tumor.

It was just a bad proposal.

Matthew had tried to book us a weekend away, but we had a newborn baby, so Baby was along for the ride. His needy little presence did not add to the romantic atmosphere. Because babies make everything take at least an hour longer than it should, we got a late start on the road, and didn't arrive at the resort until well past eight o'clock. The cabin Matthew had rented online was mysteriously "no longer available," and we were given the keys to a "comparable" one that had the vibe of a 1980s horror movie in the making. I'm no princess, so I can handle some murder vibes, but I could not handle what came next.

There was no bathtub.

That might not sound like a big deal, but that third wheel we were carting around had very recently wrecked the lower half of my body, our bathtub at home was too tiny for me to properly soak in, and the promise of a bath was the one thing that got my postpartum self into a car for a two-hour drive to the middle of nowhere.

"What about a hot shower?" Matthew asked tentatively, and I burned him alive with the laser beams that shot out of my eyes.

"What *about* a hot shower, Matthew?"

It was past nine o'clock when we finally settled into a cabin that met my approval, and I ran a bath, locked the door, and cracked a book, not knowing the entire time that Matthew was teetering on the edge of his own breakdown.

Once I'd boiled myself for at least an hour, I joined Matthew and Baby in the living room, where a fire was roaring.

The combination of hormones and having sat in a tub of hot water for sixty minutes had caught up with me, and I instantly felt as though I was going to burn alive from the inside. "OH MY GOD," I shouted, "it's SO HOT IN HERE!"

Matthew turned the (gas) fire down a few notches, and handed me a glass of wine, which made me want to throw up. And then, he started a very long and very confusing monologue that I interrupted probably four or five times because I had no idea what was happening. What was happening was he was a sweaty, nervous wreck who wanted to ask me to marry him. I figured that last part out because suddenly, he was holding a box and saying "I want to ask you to marry me."

Several moments passed, and then he did ask me, and I said yes, and also said, "Why are you so nervous, you weirdo?!"

The proposal wasn't bad because of the cabin, or the fire, or the attempted monologue. It was terrible because I didn't need it or want it but he did it anyway.

You know why Matthew proposed to me? Because I wanted him to. I know I *just* said that I didn't want him to, but this big, loud feminist just wanted to know what it would feel like to be The Bachelorette (which, even though it's a woman picking a spouse from a sea of hair-gelled Ken Dolls, still requires that the dude propose). A part of me wanted the ring, and the proposal, and the story.

And a part of Matthew still felt like it was his responsibility to perform that part of a relationship. When I saw his sweaty, nervous face, I thought . . . why? Why was this his job? This is a shy, sweet man who once left Dairy Queen with a completely blank cake because he didn't want to bother the staff with writing Happy 4th of July on it. Why does the responsibility for a big, romantic overture fall onto him when I'm so obviously better at it? This man had recently seen a human being emerge from my vagina. We had, with the birth of this child, who slept through this entire debacle, entwined our lives forever. We didn't need to put a ring on it; we had put a baby on it. Why was he nervous for what should really be just a conversation? Why was he awkwardly handing me a ring?

MY GRANDMOTHER REFUSED TO BUY a wedding gift for any couple until they'd been married for a full year. She also found wedding registries tasteless—is it really a gift if you've already selected it for yourself and someone else just pays for it?—so she'd send a piece of Waterford or a work of her own art after your first anniversary. No explanation, no apology. To grandma, weddings were nice parties, but they never impressed her. "Do you want a wedding," she'd lecture us, "or do you want a marriage?" The two weren't mutually exclusive, but she wanted us to know that our focus should be on the latter. Grandma was what we'd call today an "untraditional bride." She and grandpa were married during World War II, on an army base, where she had taken the train to visit my grandfather before he shipped out. She wore a suit. Two guys from the army served as their witnesses. Not even her own parents were in attendance. There is one snapshot from that day. By today's standards, where the average American wedding costs upwards of $33,000 (!!!!!) that's not much of a wedding. But by today's standards, they had one hell of a marriage. I don't think the success of a marriage can be measured in the number of years together. The duration of a marriage tells you only that they held on, but not what they held on through. My grandparents were together for several decades. They had ten pregnancies and nine living children. They built a business together, and sold the business. If they had problems, I certainly wasn't privy to them, but I knew even when I was too young to know that it mattered that they really, really *liked* each other. By the time I was old enough to know them, my grandparents were old, but they were still deeply in like. My grandfather woke up hours before my grandmother, and had her coffee ready for her when she was up. She laughed at his corny jokes, and called him out when he was being less than reasonable, coming to our defense when we complained about spending yet another day moving a pile of bricks from one side of their property to the other. They spent their retirement voluntarily living in a secluded cabin in northern Minnesota with one bedroom and a semi-functioning TV.

I have always enjoyed weddings. As a child, I cried at nearly every wedding I attended. I was at least ten to fifteen years younger than most of my McInerny cousins, and because we were raised Catholic, several of them were married shortly after they graduated college. I cried at Becky's wedding, when I was five, in part because I caught her smoking in the bathroom and was certain she had instantly contracted cancer. I cried at Susie's wedding, in part because I saw her groom drinking beers in the parking lot and knew that it wasn't a good thing. I cried at Patty's wedding, when I was thirteen, in part because my parents had idolized Patty, and it felt like watching a movie of my future life. I would be a vibrant, glowing bride. My father would dance with me to a Frank Sinatra song; my groom would look at me like I was a piece of pizza and he a drunk college student. I sensed at a young age that the wedding itself was not as important as what the wedding symbolized. Not the coming together of two lives in eternal commitment, but just the simple fact that every wedding is a stake in time. They are not more important or less important than any other moment, they are simply anointed as special. These moments are treated like they're of a limited quantity, gold coins you spend just by being alive.

It's that anointing that has made weddings absolutely bonkers. Weddings come with enormous pressure to be beautiful, to be happy, to be a perfectly choreographed play performed in front of hundreds of people. If a day is special, shouldn't you have all the mason jars you want? The extra covers for the rental chairs? At least a dozen friends and frenemies in coordinating dresses to do your bidding for months beforehand? I have attended very few weddings that don't have a strong undercurrent of familial tension, or at least one crisis involving a hand-lettered chalkboard. For every big, fancy wedding I attend, I think, "This is so great!" and also, "I would never do any of this."

And yet, the day after Matthew's sweet and confusing proposal, I was walking through the lodge at our resort planning a "small weekend getaway wedding" for 150 of our closest friends and family. Each invitee would rent a little cabin, and we'd spend the weekend brunching and lunching and marrying. It sounded simple enough, and planned far enough in advance that it wouldn't be stressful or annoying. What would it cost? Who knows! But after two non-traditional weddings with Aaron, I was ready to bride out.

Except, as the wedding inched closer, and our plans remained as vague as they were the day I booked the space, I realized two things:

1. I had zero interest in planning, hosting, or performing a wedding.

2. We had zero money to be hosting this kind of thing.

Free advice: when you tell your fiancé that you think you should cancel the wedding, really think through your wording beforehand so it doesn't sound like "I don't want to marry you." I *did* want to marry Matthew; I just didn't want a wedding. I wanted a marriage. We could have both, but one version would cost us thousands of dollars and require people to spend *their* time and money witnessing something that would be nothing but pageantry. Matthew and I are raising four kids together in a house we bought. It seemed kinda silly for me to wear white and take a symbolic walk down the aisle to a life we'd already started.

I didn't want a wedding. I wanted a marriage. And health insurance.

In late June, we invited some friends and family over for brunch. We'd had our house for almost a year, and a baby for seven months, and most of our friends and family hadn't seen either because we were always carting the other three to extracurriculars.

We billed it as a housewarming/meet-the-baby party, and sent out a Paperless Post invite. When our guests arrived in our back-yard, we had a quick wedding ceremony, ate doughnuts, drank orange juice and coffee and champagne, and started our marriage. My sister was the officiant. Ralph was going to walk me down the aisle but instead he made me carry him. The day before, I found an orange jumpsuit at Banana Republic for $27, and it fit perfectly.

We didn't invite anyone from out of town, we didn't tell anyone in advance aside from a few family members. That way, nobody would have to feel bad about missing it, right?

Wrong.

It turns out a lot of people have a lot of feelings about other people's weddings. They would like a heads-up that they're being invited to a wedding and not just a regular brunch that they'd skip in favor of a weekend at the cabin or their nephew's soccer game. Not being invited to the wedding feels like a personal slight and in-cites a grudge they will never let go of. I can appreciate that feeling and validate it but also do not understand it at all. A wedding is just *one* day. *One day* in (hopefully) thousands that will make up a mar-riage. And while it's beautiful to be there to witness these big happy days, a wedding is not the most important part of a marriage or a friendship or any relationship.

Aaron and I were married on December 3, 2011. His funeral was on December 3, 2014. Both were attended by more people than either of us had anticipated. People we hadn't seen since the wed-ding were there for the funeral. People who stood up as our wedding party disappeared from our daily lives.

Between our wedding and Aaron's funeral, we had over a thou-sand days together. Some of those days he had chemo or radiation, some of those days I came home to find him on the floor, having a seizure. Those were the special days that we navigated on our own.

It was a sadder version of *The Great Gatsby*, because everyone *knew* Aaron was going to die and also Aaron wasn't a fraud.

We didn't need people to show up for the wedding, we needed them to show up for life.

I am not the most reliable person to show up for the traditionally special days. I send wedding gifts about two years after the ceremony not for my grandmother's cynical reason but because I just forget. I have skipped my friends' weddings because the travel was too expensive, or because I just didn't want to go. And I don't feel bad about it, because when life gets hard and real and you need someone? I'm pretty dang good at showing up.

What I've Learned from Arguing on the Internet

A list of things I've learned from arguing on the Internet:

Please fill this out and mail it to me if you've learned anything, because all I've gotten from these arguments is an elevated heart rate.

Don't Read
the Comments

My sister Meghan is nine years older than me, which is a detail I like to reinforce because she is in another decade of life and people often ask "Which one of you is older?" I blame that on their poor vision, and on the fact that I was a lifeguard for five years and the sun is the devil. Anyway, my older sister Meghan is, like many firstborn daughters, the one who keeps her shit together. Meghan blazed the trail for her three younger siblings. Even when she was in the midst of her many rebellious years, she was a high achiever who tempered things like dropping out of college at eighteen with being an eighteen-year-old with a full-time, salaried career managing people twice her age. She'd already gotten her nose pierced, been tattooed, and cohabitated before I was even out of high school, so there was hardly anything left for me to do that would irk my parents.

I, on the other hand, was born a people pleaser. It's not a diagnosis that doctors typically include in your medical records, but I bet if you went back in time to Hennepin County Medical Center in 1982, you'd see a giant baby just trying to make everyone as comfortable as possible, just laying there not crying or making a fuss, apologizing for needing a diaper change, the usual. I kept journals throughout my childhood, a continuous documentation of the ways I feared falling short of the expectations of my parents, teachers, family members, or even complete strangers.

> **I just feel like I could be doing more with my life.**
> **—DECEMBER 28, 1992**

A fun note about that excerpt is that it was written on my tenth birthday, when I treated myself not only to the customary birthday can of Coca-Cola Classic, but to an unflinching evaluation of my decade on Earth.

That diary entry could just have easily been pulled from my current journal, which is why I was so appalled when my sister told me that she wished she were more like me because I "just do whatever I want and don't care what anyone thinks."

I know she's nine years older than me and moved out of our family house before I was done with middle school, but *have we met*? I have spent over thirty years caring deeply about what people think of me, even if their opinions are not worth thinking about.

One of the coolest things about being a person who creates things for a living is that each time you put a piece of yourself out into the world, you are holding it up for the criticisms of other people. And one of the coolest things about being a person who creates things for a living in this digital era is that these criticisms are widely available to you. You don't need to wait for some professional critic to catch wind of your book or podcast or blog, you just need an internet connection and enough self-hatred and free time to actually read the comments.

You don't even need to be a creative to be treated to this. No matter what you do in this world, our culture and our technology means that we are treated to a nonstop barrage of "feedback," which is a sanitized way of saying "opinions," which is a nice way of saying "trolling." Maybe it will come in the form of a not-compliment from an acquaintance on Facebook, who liked your old haircut way better. Maybe your local newspaper will cover the event you've been working hard on for months, and the people with whom you share a ZIP code will unleash a torrent of "just an opinion, but . . ." all over your work. Most of the comments will be positive, but it doesn't matter. Because you will absorb the one negative comment, commit it to memory, marinate in it for a few long hours, and take it as the gospel truth.

I cannot tell you what any of the positive reviews of my book or podcast say. But I can tell you that one of the people who gave my book a three-star rating on Amazon gave five stars and a glowing review . . . to a snowbrush. My book about my dead husband? Three stars. A snowbrush? Five.

There is no need for me to know the contents of her other reviews, or to know her name (Lisa D.). But I do.

Here is the thing about the bad reviews. They didn't like my book and that hurt my feelings. Here is the thing about everything bad anyone has ever said to you or about you: they didn't like you or the thing you made and that hurt your feelings. You could have been someone else, or made something else, something more to their liking, and you know what? Someone else would have had something to criticize about it. You cannot escape.

I love my first book, but not everyone does. I love my podcast, but not everyone wants to listen to a podcast about the worst things that can happen in a life. I love myself, but not everyone wants to be friends with me or agrees with my politics. Not everyone will like you! And that's okay!

I think I understand where my sister was coming from in her envy of my devil-may-care lifestyle. The fear of "feedback" kept me from trying things for ages. If I couldn't guarantee my own perfection, then why try something new? Reading internet comments or Amazon reviews now is like opening up the imaginary hell that used to keep me from trying new things. Just the *idea* of having someone openly dislike me or my work held me back. It kept me in a cubicle writing tweets for brands, tweets that nobody would ever know came from my brain and my fingers. It kept me from sharing my ideas or striving for anything at all.

That is harder for me to know than the fact that my book did not live up to Lisa D.'s expectations. I am going to let you in on a secret that my past self could have really used: it doesn't *matter*. I know your mom told you this a million times in the past, but she was right and so am I, plus, I'm a mom now. So I'm double right. Ninety-nine percent of the feedback you get—or fear getting—is of no consequence. There are worse things in life than not being liked, or trying something and failing, and one of them is complacency. A world where we receive zero criticism is a world where we are not contributing, where we are living at the very baseline of our abilities. It is a world where I am not doing the work that fuels me. It is a world where I am smaller for the comfort of others, and for my own safety. So Lisa D. didn't love my book. So your mother doesn't like the way you parent your children. So your friend in the mom group thinks your new hair color is just wrong. Okay! Their opinions are valid representations of their own experiences. You can take them for what they are worth, and not take them on as your personal motto.

My sister and I own matching necklaces that say Zero Fucks. These are aspirational necklaces for each of us, because as I have explained to you, I give so many fucks. I'm unlikely to ever go from giving all the fucks to giving zero fucks, and I'm okay with that. I just want to be a person who can be judicious with her fucks, and a person who swears less so I'm going to write frick from now on because Ralph starts kindergarten soon and he knows way too many four-letter words. Whatever your personal Amazon review is, I invite you to not read it. I heretofore invite you to the Zen practice of not reading the comments. I invite you to not give equal weight and consideration to all the "feedback" that is made available to you, however tempting it is to reinforce your core belief that you are a talentless pile of garbage. I invite you to consider the feedback of people who challenge you and respect you, and not confuse criticism of your work as criticism of who you are. I invite you to get a C+ on something and say "Well, I tried!" And then try again later.

Could I be doing more with my life? The answer at age ten was yes, because I wasn't doing much. The answer at age thirty-five is also yes, even though I'm doing a lot. You can always do more. But your goal shouldn't be to have the longest to-do list, or the longest been-done list, but to have a list of things you feel good about doing. The goal should be to do things you would do whether or not anyone was going to comment on them.

I have been a writer since I could hold a pencil, long before we documented our entire existences on tiny computers we stored in our pockets. I filled notebooks and floppy disks with my words; I littered the internet with blogs that never even had one reader. Some of my best writing is in places that nobody else will ever see, note-books I scribbled in just after waking up, or before falling asleep, or in the notes app on my phone while the plane was taking off and I wasn't allowed to be on my laptop.

They're words that were written for nobody else, written just the way I lived them. You don't have to like them or give them a good review. And I don't have to read the comments.

Chapter Thirty-Seven

35

I have never loved my birthday. Birthday people—the kind who insist on celebrating for a week or a month, who drag groups of friends who have never co-mingled out for a celebratory dinner where the check is split thirty-six different ways even though three of those people drank like ten cocktails and ordered steak, and five of them drank water and ate side salads—those people confuse me. And they annoy me, honestly. I may love you deeply and truly, but I am not devoting a month of the calendar to celebrating your birth. Even if I gave birth to you, it's excessive.

My birthday is three days after Christmas—the celebratory no-man's-land where everyone you know is burned out from the holidays but also trying to conserve their energy to thrash on New Year's Eve. When your birthday falls over Winter Break in Minnesota, you know that your invites are going to have a twenty percent RSVP rate, tops. Even if my birthday had fallen in a great month—September, for example—I'd have still hated it. Birthdays meant presents and opening them in front of people made me sick. I was so afraid I wouldn't seem grateful enough that I couldn't even enjoy the act of opening a gift. I can't even remember to buy my best friend a birthday card. I have been best friends with Dave Gilmore, Jr. since 2001, and I have never remembered his birthday. I'll call him on any other day, buy gifts for him for no reason, but if the only successful measure of a friendship was getting a card in the mail within even a week of his special day? Our friendship would be an abject failure.

Aaron *loved* his birthday. All birthdays. He prided himself on knowing his friends' birthdays, on finding them excellent gifts, on celebrating the crap out of them. He knew I hated my birthday, but he didn't hate it. He loved it, because he loved birthdays and he loved me. When I turned thirty, Aaron was in the hospital recovering from his second brain surgery. I was almost nine months pregnant, and we were passing his time in the hospital the way we always did: laying together in a tiny hospital bed built for one, watching shows on his laptop. When the scheduler called to let him know that his surgery would take place early in the morning on December 26, Aaron hung up the phone, dejected, and then threw it across the room. I'd never seen him angry, and I assumed he was afraid. "It's okay," I whispered into his chest, gripping him close to me, "you'll be okay." "I'm going to miss your fucking birthday. I'll be in the fucking hospital," he choked out, wiping fat tears from his giant green eyes. I assured him I didn't give a shit about my birthday, but he shook his head. "*I* give a shit about your birthday," he insisted. I was planning on having my ideal birthday in the hospital with him. But on my birthday a few friends showed up to join us and Aaron insisted that they take me out for dinner. I didn't want to leave him, but he was pushy, so I went, promising to be back soon.

It wasn't dinner they were taking me out for. It was to a movie. And an entire theater filled with our friends and family, and a screening of my favorite movie, *Dumb & Dumber*. "NORA IS 30," screamed the marquee. "Do you like it?" he texted me. "I love it." I replied.

I haven't celebrated my birthday since Aaron died. Time takes on a new meaning when you lose someone you love, especially if that person was young. Each birthday has brought me closer to the age that Aaron was when he died, each birthday reminds me how he is frozen in time, forever thirty-five.

Now, I am thirty-five. I am thirty-five. I am thirty-five. I am the age Aaron was when he died.

How would it feel to know this was my last year on Earth? To look at our son and know that I wouldn't be there to watch him grow up? To know that my life was ending, surely and painfully? These thoughts have always been too hot to touch, but to avoid them forever seems gross, like a privilege I haven't earned.

I am currently in the midst of my midlife crisis. I'm not trying to be cute about it, either. My dad died at sixty-four, so I could very easily be over fifty percent through my run on this planet. Both my father and Aaron were talented and generous humans who died with a lot of unrealized dreams and potential still tucked away inside of them. Unlike our souls, or all of the things that end up in our estate sales, that potential does not live on; it evaporates into nothingness. My father's passion wasn't to write fitness infomercials. In my office, I have a box of all the writing he wanted to do. There are piles and piles of half-written manuscripts and brilliant ideas scribbled on scrap paper, an entire box of unrealized dreams. Aaron's Best Life wasn't sitting through a status meeting about a website for a brand-new, highly innovative livestock feed. He loved to make things just to make them—posters and T-shirts and logos for companies I never started. I don't know what more they would have done, like what the famous Pinterest quotes ask of us, if they knew they could not fail. I don't know what they would have created if they'd only had the time, or the money. I just know that the only way to honor these two men and their too-short lives is to make the most of mine.

Midlife crises get a bad rap. Probably because they're associated with mediocre men purchasing muscle cars and clinging desperately to their fading youth. This midlife crisis of mine didn't manifest itself as a sports car and a younger husband. I actually got a minivan and an older husband! I will admit that there are some traditional elements to my midlife crisis: I got some more tattoos, I bought a very expensive road bike with a current Cost Per Use of $100. I considered signing up for a triathlon, and I got laser hair removal even though I was nowhere close to being seen naked by anyone who wasn't a medical professional during that point of my life.

The real hallmark of this midlife crisis hardly makes it seem like a crisis at all. I'm obsessed with making the most of mine. I'm focused on doing as much as I can, with trying as much as I can, with kicking over as many rocks as I can in case there is a scrap of life that I haven't yet lived. This is how I honor Aaron and my father: by making sure their deaths aren't a black hole that sucked me in, but the spark I needed to be able to burn brighter.

I did not know how to do that at first because I'd spent nearly ten years of my life in various cubicles, and the twenty-some years before that doing all of the things I was supposed to be doing: getting As, collecting Gold Stars, getting promoted at work, moving forward in all of the ways I'd been expected to, and in ways I hadn't been: scheduling chemo, administering nausea meds, carrying a grown man to and from our bedroom.

But now what? When The Game of Life (a truly awful and depressing board game, by the way) decides that your husband dies of brain cancer and leaves you alone to raise your toddler, where do you go from there? Do you pass Go and attempt to collect social security? Am I mixing up my board game metaphors?

IT'S NOT ABOUT LIVING as though everything is *fine*. Nothing is ever just fine, unless you are a criminally boring person or a complete liar. It's about facing whatever darkness looms over you: your suffering, your sorrow, your sickness, and still putting one foot in front of the other. It's not scaling mountains and high-fiving eagles, it's switching careers when you're ten years into one that sucks out your soul during standard business hours, Monday to Friday. It's going on a first date for the first time in forty-three years, when you haven't bought new underwear since the mid-nineties. It's knowing that the little light of yours shines even brighter when you're in total darkness.

I don't expect to be great at everything. And I don't need to be. I can take a few piano lessons and quit if it's not for me. I can start a podcast or a nonprofit with no experience and see if anyone cares to listen. I can learn to meditate regularly, and then quit. Then try to start again. I can try to get to know Jesus again, and apologize for all the bad things I said about his dad when Aaron died. I can march in the streets for our immigrant neighbors and hold the hand of the old man next to me when the plane's turbulence makes us both so scared that we wipe tears from our eyes when we land safely in Minneapolis. I can fall in love with a new man without falling out of love with Aaron. I can fail if I have to. Or go back to a cube if things get desperate. Because the worst thing that can happen isn't that I die. I'm *going* to die. Unlike death, the truly sad and devastating thing is avoidable and fixable. It's spending our time here trying to avoid the depths of misery, and in the process, missing out on the climb to happiness. It's spending our time in the middle, being alive without living. The cure comes from being pulled against our will from the comfort of a monotonous life. It doesn't matter if you're thirty or sixty, or how much of your life is actually left on the clock. It's never too early or late for a good midlife crisis.

Chapter Thirty-Eight

Greatness and Goodness

W hat the FUCK are you even talking about?"

I had just landed in California when Matthew called. It was the middle of the workday for him, so I expected he was calling between meetings to say hello, to tell me that one of our kids was sick and needed to be picked up early, or to tell me he found my phone charger—the one I couldn't find this morning—in a very obvious place, the moment I'd left.

Instead, he was calling to tell me that his brother Michael was dead.

And for all the time I spend discussing difficult topics, the best thing I could come up with for this moment was "What the FUCK are you even talking about?" Blame it on the shock. The sort-of shock. It's always going to be shocking when someone dies, especially when they were planning to come over for dinner soon. It's going to be shocking even if it's not totally a shock. Nobody—not even Michael—expected him to live a long life. But we didn't expect *this*. We didn't expect his parents to find him dead on his couch the day they returned from a long, leisurely cruise. Michael was only forty-two years old. He had no business being dead.

Michael was Matthew's older brother. Even in photos from their childhood, you can tell that life was not easy for Michael, that it was a puzzle he doesn't have all the pieces for. He is always standing, wraithlike, on the periphery. Hardly, if ever, smiling. Doing his best to appear comfortable.

I have known people like Michael. We all have. And if you haven't known them you have at least seen them. And probably judged them. Michael had long hair that we all wished he would cut and plugs in his earlobes that were hard to look at. His shoulders slumped. His speech was slow. His feet shuffled. His nails were long and stained with nicotine. His interests were esoteric. He was in this world, but not a part of it. He was a bystander, an observer.

Mentally, he was doing his best as an alien visitor to this strange planet of ours, trying his best to learn our customs and adhere to our many confusing norms. The day we met, we searched for common conversational ground. He asked if I liked horror movies. I said no. Did I like *Japanese* horror movies he wondered? Also, no. He asked if I liked music, and I said yes! Did I like punk music? Only if you count Paramore and Blink-182, I answered. He did not.

Physically, Michael was forty-two going on seventy. He had struggled for years with severe mental illness that made being alive difficult in every sense. He'd attempted suicide multiple times, he'd been admitted to several psych wards and been prescribed so much lithium he had gone into renal failure. The medications he took to keep his illnesses at bay made him sleepy, made him gain weight, and came with a list of warnings that made it clear his life would not be a long one. It was hard for him to connect with people, hard for him to build relationships, hard for him to work and maintain an independent life, but he managed. He had a part-time job. He had his own apartment. He was proud to say that he had never had to go back to a psych ward after moving to Minnesota. He wanted to be well enough to own a dog again.

He did all of this—the stuff most of us take for granted—with love and support from his mother, who kept him on top of doctor's appointments. Who checked in with him every day. Who knew before she even opened the door to his apartment that day, that her oldest son was dead.

Like every huge life plot twist, everything after the phone call about Michael's death was a blur. By the time I got on a plane to come home, the Grief Machine was already plugging along the way it does: with a to-do list. There was an apartment to clean out. An obituary to write. Family to call. Accounts to settle. And a memorial of some kind to plan.

I have spent a lot of time imagining my own funeral. I've done it since I was a kid. Probably because when you're raised Catholic, going to funerals is a part of your social life. Maybe some little girls spent their days planning their wedding day, their Big Special Party. Not this little girl. I was busy thinking about the LAST party I'd ever throw. The music, the general run of the show, the life-size cutouts of me at various life stages that attendees could pose with for photo ops.

Michael was not such a planner. He never wanted a funeral. He wanted an Irish wake at his favorite place in Madison, Wisconsin. So his extended family tried to give him that. We drove five hours to sit in a basement banquet room for a late lunch and beers. We poured beers and ordered nachos and let our kids run wild.

I ran my fingers over the childhood photos his mother had spread across an adjacent table and felt my heart swell with sadness for Childhood Michael and Teenager Michael, two beautiful boys who seemed to know that they would reach adulthood broken, if at all. I cried for that little boy who doesn't know the darkness that is coming for him in adulthood, for that teenager whose dreams will go unrealized. Not because he is a bad person, but because he lost the genetic lottery, the one that says in an Oprah voice:

"You get a normal life and die in your sleep at eighty-eight!"

"You get brain cancer and die at thirty-five!"

"And you die at forty-two from complications from the many medications that helped manage your debilitating mental illnesses!"

I've been to many funerals, and memorials, and plenty that were very non-traditional. But I know that you're supposed to say something. Someone is supposed to say something. Not something perfect, but something to summarize a dead person. Something that highlights his best qualities, something that proves that he was here, that he mattered, that he will be missed. Near the end of the afternoon, Michael and Matthew's mother, through her tears, thanked everyone for coming. We raised our glasses. And there was—at least to me—a long moment of quiet, the moment where someone was supposed to say that something that would unleash all the sad, that would let us all cry and wipe our noses on our sleeves and let us all know that he was real, even if he was imperfect.

But who? Who was going to do this? Michael's brothers shrank into themselves. His cousins did not stir.

His uncle stood up, and I relaxed.

Someone was saying something.

It was a short joke—not an inappropriate one, not a mean one, just . . . a joke. And a toast.

We clinked glasses and made eye contact. "To Michael."

And that quiet returned, waiting for someone to fill it.

Someone should say something, I thought, and nudged Matthew, who looked like he would break into a thousand pieces if he opened his mouth.

And then it passed. The moment of quiet was over. Our nachos arrived.

We ate.

We talked about the weather and the NCAA tournament.

We said good-bye the Midwestern way—forty minutes of small talk standing in the doorway—and walked to our cars.

It was over. And nothing had been said.

Back at the hotel, we retreated to our rooms, emotionally congested and ready for bed at six p.m., everything that hadn't been said spinning around in our heads.

That night I held Michael's little brother, the man I'm now married to, and we cried and cried. Quietly, because we were sharing a room with our children, and there were two additional humans in our bed. We cried because nobody said anything. Because we didn't say anything. Because what do you say when a complicated person dies a complicated death after a complicated life?

It was hard to fall asleep that night, and when we woke up, the sky in Madison was gray and heavy. We gathered our things, packed the kids up in the minivan, and headed back to Minneapolis.

It was a quiet ride. I thought about Michael.

I thought about the children I'm raising with Matthew. About how there is so much life ahead of them, and we have not a clue and no control over what awaits them.

I thought about how we speak to our kids, and how I try to make sure that they all know two important things about themselves, and about other people: that there is greatness and goodness in all of us.

It is a simple idea I got from a conversation with my friend Damon, who is an amazing dad. I hold our children's faces in my hands and tell them they have greatness inside of them, and goodness, too. I remind them that greatness and goodness are two things they are meant to uncover in themselves and find in other people. I don't know what to tell them about why life is so much harder for some people than it is for others because I just don't know. I hope they grow up to be gentle with themselves and with others.

When I cry for Michael, it is because he had greatness inside of him, and goodness, too. Michael was unapologetically himself, and I loved that. I loved Michael, just as immediately as I loved his little brother. I love love love people who are themselves, who love what they love with no apologies. Michael didn't mind that I didn't share his love of horror movies or punk music. We connected over what we did have in common: liberal politics and the family I was being invited into. Though his anxiety prevented him from doing much outside of his apartment, he was the first to arrive at the hospital when my second son was born. He was the first to congratulate me on our engagement. "It will be so nice to call you my sister," he told me, "I love you."

I should have said how brave Michael was, to live in a body whose chemistry was so difficult, in a world that doesn't understand people like him. In a world where people use words like "schizo" or "bipolar" as a casual adjective, a way to describe something that doesn't work quite right, or someone who doesn't quite act normally, like they aren't actual diagnoses that real people struggle with.

Michael did his best. And he did it with a kind heart.

He had greatness inside of him, and goodness, too.

Somebody should have said it sooner. So I'm saying it now.

Chapter Thirty-Nine

She Persisted

She was warned.
She was given an explanation.
Nevertheless, she persisted.
—MITCH McCONNELL

think it's safe to say that even the most diehard Republicans wouldn't get a Mitch McConnell tattoo scrawled into their forearm. But that's what makes me a true McConnell fan: I'm willing to go there.

I am not *actually* a McConnell fan, but don't let that stop you from reading this chapter! I'm not one of those mean people who points out that he looks like a turtle. I don't think that's a helpful way to talk about our country's leaders. He looks like a *sea* turtle, which is an important specification to make. Sea turtles are much cuter than freshwater turtles.

Mitch is also the author of the words above. Which were said not about a petulant granddaughter, but about his colleague Elizabeth Warren. The Mitch tattoo on my right forearm is an abbreviated version of this slight, just the last two words in a script hand-lettered by my friend Chelsea Brink and etched into my skin by my friend Emily Snow: she persisted.

nevertheless, she persisted.

she persisted.

Mitch was not trying to compliment Elizabeth, by the way. He wasn't applauding her tenacity or her drive. The meaning of the words he chose was clear to any woman who has ever encountered any friction in a male-dominated world, and he didn't have to say it explicitly to get his meaning across: "Lady, just *shut up* already."

A year before, I didn't know who Mitch McConnell was. He'd been the Senate Majority leader since 2015, and a senator since 1985, and I don't think I'd heard his name until a little election happened in 2016, and suddenly, I really and truly *cared* about politics.

I have to also admit that I have been able to spend most of my life blissfully unaware of the political issues that surround us, which I learned a few years ago is referred to as *privilege*. I didn't really have to care too much about how terrible the world was because as a middle-class white girl from the Midwest, it was never that terrible for me personally. And the things that were, I was willing to ignore or explain away.

Once Aaron died, my view changed. I had rage. I had enough rage to address the fact that our country was in real trouble. I did this in very productive ways, like getting into Twitter fights with idiotic strangers. I donated money, I showed up to march for women's rights and against the Muslim ban. I got to know my state representative and paid attention to what my Congress people were doing in Washington. I called out bad behavior when I saw it online and in person, even when it made people uncomfortable. This is . . . not a lot of work, honestly, so I don't expect to be patted on the back for any of it. This is pretty basic civic participation.

Truly, most of us aren't world changers. Most of us aren't going to end up on the cover of a magazine or hold elected office. That can make it feel like our words and actions don't count for much, or that there isn't much that we can do. There's something to be said for persistence. For small acts that can add up to something bigger.

Mitch's words struck a chord. Not just with me, but with tons of women around the country. I've got a little secret for you: a lot of people don't *love* persistent women. A lot of people don't *love* women with contrary opinions or strong convictions. A lot of people would prefer if we just kept those thoughts to ourselves, if we accepted the reasons given and heeded their warnings. Because we've all had a Mitch or seven in our lives. We've all worked with, or been with, or are related to a guy like this. We've all been hushed or told we're being hormonal. Many of us have believed it. We spent years trying to make ourselves smaller, trying to make ourselves more likable. We thought if we just did what we were told, then maybe we'd be accepted, maybe we'd be successful. Maybe a hot guy would like us!

My friends and I created a Facebook event to get our tattoos. Because I am sometimes embarrassingly stupid, I made the event public, and thousands of people clicked the "interested" box. I know that's the laziest form of RSVP, the equivalent of the "like" button, but really, hundreds of women showed up for this tattoo. Chelsea put the design on her website, and women around the country and the world brought it into their neighborhood tattoo shop and joined the persisterhood. I have spotted them out in the wild several times, and it's always a thrill. We wear them on our forearms, our wrists, our ankles, our ribs. Some are visible only to us, and some we show off to the world. These are dismissive words turned into wise words, reminding us to keep speaking up, showing up, and pissing off ancient sea turtles. To keep persisting.

Chapter Forty

Yes, And

We take up two booths at the Waffle House. We'd take up more, but those are the last two tables available, so we pull up a high chair for Baby at one table, tack an extra chair to the end of the second table, and jam the kids in as close as they can fit to one another while still maintaining minimal arm function. Matthew and I join Aaron's sister, Nikki, as perpetual servers. We pass plates back and forth across the tables, making sure that Ralph's rejected hash browns end up on Gabe's plate, that Josie's extra ham makes it to Ian, that Ian's extra waffle makes it to Sophie, and everyone's scraps make it to Baby. Mae Mae and Opa are doing what grandparents do: pretending to follow along with seven different disjointed conversations about cartoons they've never seen, toys they've never heard of, and friends they've never met. When they have a moment to speak, they use it to heap praise upon each of their grandchildren, no matter how much syrup they've poured onto their plates or how many glasses of chocolate milk they've spilled.

These two tables are filled with people who used to be strangers and are now family.

My current husband, Matthew, does not love being called my current husband, but it's the most accurate way to describe him. Saying "my husband" is true, but it doesn't include the fact that my marriage to Aaron didn't end just because he died of brain cancer. Though he's the second man I've married, calling Matthew my "second husband" makes it sound like he's a consolation prize. He is, however, currently my husband, and he is currently sitting next to my sister-in-law, Nikki. Nikki is not my biological sister or married to Matthew's brother. Nikki is Aaron's sister. She is feeding pieces of waffle to my baby; Mae Mae and Opa—Aaron's parents—have brought belated Christmas gifts for Matthew's oldest children, Ian and Sophie. Nikki's daughter, Josie, is begging to carry Baby to the car. Nikki's son, Gabe, is cutting Ralph's waffle for him.

Ralph is licking the table, the coffee is God awful, and I am purely, completely happy. I also spent last night sleeplessly creeping from room to room in our Airbnb, checking to make sure that everyone in our family was still breathing (they were).

After Aaron's funeral, when the temperatures in Minnesota took their annual dive below zero, I packed a suitcase for me and Ralph and headed to Nikki's house in Arizona. In under four hours, Ralph and I had left the land of snowdrifts and pine for a world of dust and cactus. I marveled at this, as I stood on the sidewalk outside the Phoenix airport, holding our coats under my arm and sweating slightly. How mind boggling to think that on the same day, in the same country, we can experience an arid desert and an arctic prairie. Stranger, still, that life can and does unfold in each of them, each inhospitable in their own ways. What would freeze solid in Minnesota blooms steadily in Arizona. What would wither in the

Arizona sun withstands the Minnesota cold. The shock of Aaron's death had blown a gaping, invisible hole in the center of my being. Life may be continuing around me, but it would no longer continue within me. I was desert and frozen tundra. I was inhospitable to all of it.

My first trip to Arizona was meant to last a week, but when the day came to fly home, I didn't go to the airport. Instead, I laid in Josie's bed with Ralph until ten a.m., then joined Nikki on the back patio, where we sat in quiet while the kids played on the burned-out grass in their backyard. When noon struck, the white wine was cracked. After dinner, we sat in silence watching intellectually stimulating programs like *Real Housewives of Orange County*. Nikki's husband, Andrew, hovered without interrupting us. He kept our glasses full and tucked in the children. There weren't words to say or acts to complete, there was just the quiet comfort of being close to a person who loved the same person you did, who missed him as much as you do.

The first rule of Improv is *yes*. Well, *yes, and* . . . the *and* is important.

Yes is acceptance and acknowledgment of the reality you've been handed. If your stage partner says "I've made you a delicious dinner, with my grandmother's famous pickled salamanders!" you don't say, "No, you made me pork chops, which makes more sense and sounds more appetizing." You pick up a fork, *and* . . .

When your husband dies, it feels like a ridiculous scene that has been thrust upon you by some obnoxious idiot, and it is. You did not get to choose this, but here it is, in all its horrifying glory. *Yes* is nothing but acceptance.

And is where the good part happens. The good part is a conjunction? You bet it is. Because *and* is about possibility and opportunity. *And* includes *what is* and makes room for *what could be*. *And* doesn't require you to love the situation, or to like the situation; it just requires you to live.

My default reaction to Aaron's death was not "yes, and . . ." it was "yes, but . . ."

"Yes, Aaron died, but please don't pity me."

"Yes, I'm a widowed mother, but I can't talk about it deeply with anyone who loves me."

"Yes, I'm very sad theoretically, but I can't express it in any way."

My expectations for what life and life with grief were supposed to look like put me constantly on the defensive: wanting to prove myself and my grief, wanting to hide it away. If *and* brings you possibility, *but* cuts it right off at the knees. I didn't know that when I met Matthew.

"I love Matthew, but I'm in love with Aaron," I told myself and anyone else who knew about the relationship.

"I love Matthew, and I love Aaron," I should have said.

The change of three letters makes all the difference: in how that reads, in how it feels, in how it *lives*. Because *but* makes our hearts and possibilities so much smaller than they are. *And* is where it's at.

And is where I am now.

And does not deny the past, or the pain. *And* makes room for it, in a way that *but* does not. And allows for the future, too.

And makes room for the multitudes included in all our experiences. And those two tables at Waffle House—our family—is full of *and*. Aaron's parents are Mae Mae and Opa to all of our children. They love Matthew and they miss their son. Matthew's oldest children have a life and a family at our house, and outside of it. It's beautiful to watch Ralph be so loved and doted on by Matthew, and it's tragic that he will never get to know Aaron.

Yes, I have a life I love, and a life I miss.

Yes, I am filled with happiness and gratitude, and with an eternal ache.

Yes, Matthew is my husband and the love of my life. And so is Aaron.

Yes, we have all been broken before. And yes, we could break all over again.

The years will roll on. More joy. More pain. More possibility. More yes. More and.

More.

Acknowledgments

This book is here because I did everything all on my own, as always, with no help from anyone. Thanks for nothing.

KIDDING!

This book is here because of Jess Regel and Julia Cheiffetz and Carrie Thornton. Because of Aaron Purmort and Matthew Hart and Dave Gilmore and Hannah Meacock Ross and Lindsay Wenner and Hans Buetow and Moe Richardson. Because of Ian, and Sophie, and Ralph, and Baby. Because of Mae Mae and Opa and Nikki and Andrew and Shari and Jim and Madame and Patrick and Austin and Meghan. Because of Steve McInerny.

This book is here because so many people—strangers, even!—gave a rip about me and my family and the work that I do. Because so many of you are living your own complicated life and love stories right now, and *get it*.

Thank you.

ABOUT THE AUTHOR

Nora McInerny is a reluctant expert in difficult conversations. As the host of American Public Media's Gracie Award–winning podcast *Terrible, Thanks for Asking*, Nora brings empathy and wit to tough subjects. Nora is a contributor to Elle.com, Cosmopolitan.com, the *Minneapolis Star Tribune*, Buzzfeed, Time.com, Slate, and Vox, where she's often tapped for her essay pieces highlighting the emotional landscape and humor in complex topics, like the financial impacts of healthcare and grief in a digital age. She founded the nonprofit Still Kickin and the Hot Young Widows Club, an online group of people who have lost their significant other.